Tourette Syndrome and Music

Discovering Peace Through Rhythm and Tone

David R. Aldridge

Foreword by
Loire Cotler MA, CMT

Rollinson Publishing Co.
Los Angeles, California

Published 2014 by Rollinson Publishing Co.
Los Angeles, California

First Edition, First Printing 2014

www.RollinsonPublishing.com

ISBN 978-0-9852237-2-4

Production/Book Design: David R. Aldridge

Art Direction: Victoria Lopshire

Proofreading: Betsey Stephens, Victoria Lopshire

Photos: Lita D. Aldridge, Julie Collier, Rothco Press, used with permission

Photo editing: Charles T. Wegman

Excerpts from *Musicophilia: Tales of Music and the Brain* (Oliver Sacks, Knopf Doubleday, 2007) on back cover used with permission

Cover art: © Abstractus Designus - Fotolia.com

Okay, Max, it's really done now. C'mon, I'm buyin'...

Gratitude

Elden and Lolita Aldridge
Charles Aldridge, Stan Levin
- my dear family

Victoria Lopshire, Betsey Stephens, Charles T. Wegman
- my most awesome book production crewmeisters

Ken Berry, Betty Moudy, Bernard Kosc
L. Jerome Rehberg, Dick Kenny, Joe Brancato
Hal Schiff, Peter Erskine, Hank Levy, Terry Bozzio
- my path-forging teachers

Dr. Harvey Singer, Julius Wechter, Nick Ceroli
Ed Shaughnessy, Frank Zappa, Arthur Brown
- my serious lifechangers

Remo Belli, John Fitzgerald, Mike DeMenno (Remo, Inc.)
- my real-deal models for being of service

Bob Courdy, Jonah Schnel
(Southern California Tourette Syndrome Association)
- my thoughtful TSA mentors

Julie Collier (Tourettes Action UK)
- my selfless miracle worker

Marie Tran
- my I.T. savior and Mac goddess

Loire Cotler
*- my rhythmic reminder to keep
moving, singing, and being*

Dr. Oliver Sacks
*- my inspiration for setting the
neuro-musical bar as high as possible*

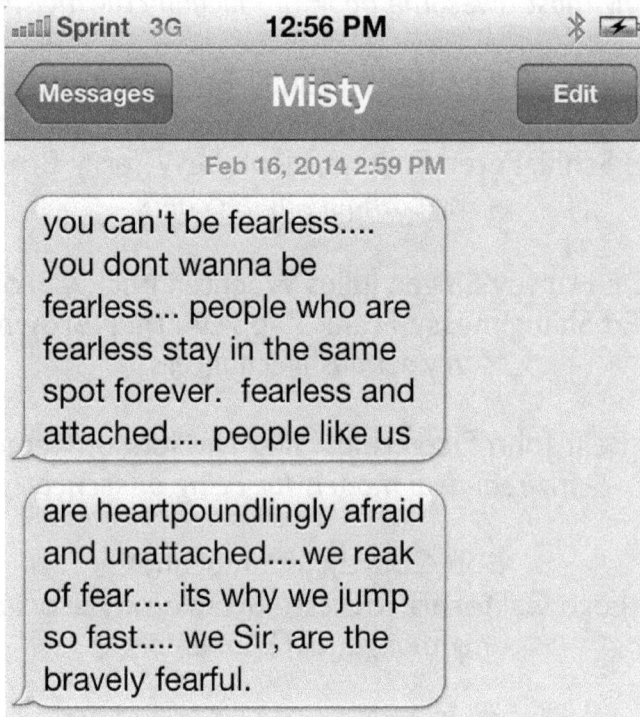

For Misty Dyan Batson

You.
woman
artist, poet
seeker of life
filler of red balloons
finder of important stuffs.

You dance like no one's watching,

You're the most brilliant writer I know,

And, you juggle.

Here... have some cake :)

Table of Contents

Table of Contents (cont'd)

**In memory of
Adam Ward Seligman**

Friend, drummer, and writing mentor

Preface

This book aims to inspire anyone with Tourette's to explore the many therapeutic benefits of music performance and listening.

For parents of those with Tourette's, you will hopefully gain insight into how music can serve to bring joy and pleasure into the lives of your children.

For family members and friends, you may better understand what someone with this disorder has to deal with in their daily living, and perhaps suggest music to them as relief.

My exploration of it was somewhat informal and improvised. To learn more about formal music therapy and to find contact information for music therapists, visit the American Music Therapy Association at www.musictherapy.org.

I also recommend Patricia Heenan's book, *Kevin and Me: Tourette Syndrome and the Magic Power of Music Therapy* (Hope Press, 2000).

For information about the national Tourette Syndrome Association, with state chapter and international links, visit www.tsa-usa.org

And remember: as with any pursuit, you really *can* have too much of a good thing. Ears are very sensitive organs, and proper volume levels and proper protection should be considered with any musical pursuits.

Foreword

Loire Cotler MA, CMT

There is a phenomenon in nature that occurs whereby something poisonous grows in the same soil as the antidote, a common example being poison ivy and jewelweed. In looking at the medicine stories of our own lives, we are often confronted with this startling proximity, that embedded within the suffering, there lies the panacea. David R. Aldridge demonstrates this holistic phenomenon so elegantly in his personal account, *Tourette Syndrome and Music: Discovering Peace Through Rhythm and Tone.*

Some of the most inspirational healing narratives teach us that curative properties are often revealed when we move toward the malady and lean into it. Aldridge takes us through his own extraordinary medicine story, which centers around a life immersed in the multidimensional world of rhythm and pulse. Undiagnosed until the age of 20, Aldridge synchronized with the musical qualities of his involuntary movement outbursts and transformed them into rhythmic beauty. His instinct to "jam with the enemy" offered tremendous relief and therapy to the torment brought on by Tourette's.

In the clinical application of music therapy, the integration of drumming into the therapeutic milieu offers a direct channel to express explosive energy, as well as to soothe and entrain the mind. Since time immemorial, traditional cultures tell us of the shaman casting off unwanted spirits using sound tools, such as the drum, voice and/or rattle. David R. Aldridge provides a moving and modern music therapy account of his heartening success, a success which culminated in his becoming a prominent musician, educator and airplane flight instructor.

This book offers a fresh perspective on the efficacy of the therapeutic and improvised applications of rhythm and tone. Herein lie valuable insights for the parent or care giver of anyone suffering from Tourette Syndrome and the importance of music therapy integration into their treatment plan.

Loire Cotler is a world-renowned rhythm vocalist, music therapist, and former music therapy professor, based in New York City. For more information on this extraordinary artist, please visit her website at www.loirevox.com

"Our nature consists in motion..."

– Blaise Pascal

Introduction

In 1992, I wrote "Rhythm Man," a short story published in *Don't Think About Monkeys* (Hope Press), which was an anthology of personal accounts written by people with Tourette Syndrome. I offered a basic look at how drumming had served as therapy for me, and for many years after that, I wanted to elaborate on how I'd benefited from drumming and talk about where the artist road had taken me.

But fear got in the way.

I dragged my heels on this book for years, scared to lay it all out on the table, scared that my livelihood as an airplane flight instructor would screech to a halt if clients knew I had Tourette's, even though I was absolutely safe and legal to fly. I was scared to open up to the world and risk everything that I was sure would follow.

<u>Absolutely</u> sure.

And then around 2009, a few things changed...

I received an e-mail from Nancy Olson, an English professor at Sacramento City College, in Sacramento, California. Nancy told me she'd assigned "Rhythm Man" as a reading assignment, and that people really enjoyed it. She sent me some moving and inspiring letters from a few students, and tears hit the pages as I realized that fear needed to be replaced with something more powerful, more constructive, and far more honest. Because honestly, I was living in between two worlds and not knowing what to do with either of them.

I started writing a draft of the book, jotting down ideas here and there, still going about it halfheartedly, until I plowed my motorcycle into the back of a truck in Los Angeles rush hour traffic. Ouch. I hurt my shoulder badly, and when I came home from the emergency room, I sat in a chair with my left arm in a cloth sling, trying to type with one hand.

I looked at the computer, and then at my drum set. I was incredibly lucky, ridiculously lucky, but I knew I was done with riding, and I knew there was clearly just one more huge thing to be done with my life... and that was to stop being afraid and share my story.

It might mean risking being able to make a living at something I had worked so hard to become, ever seeking to push the limits of Tourette's... and always thinking maybe one day, I would open up. But even with the accident, it took a bit more to get things going.

Kaikay Hwang, an elementary school nurse from Long Beach, attended an in-service for Tourette's one day, and she told me she'd met Bob Courdy, who was then president of the Southern California Chapter of the Tourette Syndrome Association. Bob actually remembered me from when I was involved with the chapter many years ago, and we started talking...

Between Kaikay and Bob, I got braver. Much braver. And, I realized it was more important to be of service and share everything than to simply ponder endlessly what might come of it. That's always a very tough part of this disorder for me.

Tourette Syndrome and Music

Still, it took five more years for this book to come to fruition, because I had two other much larger projects I was working on. I had to finish them before I committed to this one, but once I dug in, the fear faded, and my confidence in wanting to be of service came to life.

I focused on learning how to present formal drum circle and drum set demonstrations for kids with Tourette's. I framed my thoughts about a lifetime of music, of the things I'd done and all the things I wished I'd done but did not... because of fear. The important thing was that once I started moving, I kept going, and fear did not win.

I must give very special credit to Victoria Lopshire, whose beautifully critical eye in the final creative stages of this book saw how things should look. It was she who offered the sub-title, "discovering peace," which could not have more accurately summed up the message that needed sharing. Her brutal honesty about this project was exactly what I needed, every time, and she was right, every time.

/ /

If you have Tourette's, or if you are the parent or friend of someone with Tourette's, you know how difficult the road can be living with this "sudden intruder." It's a never-ending series of muscle movement surprises, a non-stop mental roller coaster that takes you on a mighty wild ride. With this story that's taken a lifetime to write, I hope to provide you with some helpful thoughts on how I've dealt with the ups and downs that color this disorder.

I grew up not knowing what caused my nervousness, and I did not receive an accurate diagnosis until I was 20. From the age of six, music was my salvation, my escape, and my enduring hope during this fourteen-year period of excruciating uncertainty. Today, I play, write, and record my own music, mostly electric jazz, and it still brings me great pleasure to relax and let the creativity flow. I also teach drumming, and I lecture about rhythm pattern theory, based on my original book series, *The Elements of Rhythm, Vols. I & II.*

I made my living for many years as a freelance magazine writer, but in 2004, I shifted direction and trained to become an airplane flight instructor. I went on to fly over 8,000 hours, teaching others how to take command of the skies. From this, I learned that it is we and we alone who let Tourette Syndrome give us limitations... but as I have also learned, sometimes it's not no easy to share all the things you know.

I strongly believe that drumming gave me the coordination and focus to master operating airplane controls, perform multi-tasking, handle the intense radio communications, and contain the often *very* challenging aspects of landing. And while I can't say that music could be this beneficial for everyone, it's certainly been the biggest help in my case.

So, that said, let me tell you about a most interesting journey, told with deepest appreciation to Nancy Olson, Kaikay Hwang, Bob Courdy, and Victoria Lopshire. Whatever benefits may come from these pages for readers, and whatever course my life takes from here, four rivers came together in synchrony to help float my boat out to sea towards the endless horizon that I now look forward to discovering with full sails and a steeled gaze.

In a *really* perfect world, I'll be bringing that boat to many distant shores and unloading some drums to tell this story with rhythm, with truth and confidence, and with a smile that's been a very long time in coming.

But honestly, I think some fear will always be there, although it seems I've been able to get a lot braver about it.

And who knows... maybe *that* really is the answer to the question, "*Will I ever fully learn to live with Tourette Syndrome?*"

Guess we'll see...

David R. Aldridge
Los Angeles, California 3-2-14

Part I

The Ride

Tourette Syndrome and Music

Chapter 1

World Interrupted

It's been almost fifty years, yet I can still clearly remember the view, looking down the steep grade of Exposition Blvd., with one foot planted on the pedal, the other resting on the ground, sizing things up and thinking, "This is gonna be pretty intense..."

In 1965, I was six years old, growing up in Austin, Texas, just a kid wanting to go fast. That particular day, I'd swapped my big, black, bulky, 3-speed Schwinn bicycle for a ride on a friend's much faster, sleeker, little red rocket. As I headed down the hill, gravity started to do its thing, complete with a nerve-wracking shimmy. Next thing I knew, I was airborne.

I landed squarely in front of a church, unconscious and scraped. I don't remember what happened to my friend's bike, but I was very lucky that the car behind me had not been going too fast. During the ambulance ride to the hospital, I asked the medics to crank up the siren. It was the loudest musical tone I'd ever caused, but it sure wouldn't be the last.

And within a month, the neck spasms began.

Over the next few months, and the course of my life, these unpredictable movements would eventually migrate without rhyme or reason all over my body, to my vocal chords, my arms, stomach, and legs. Head injury is not a prerequisite cause, but I was demonstrating the beginnings of the classic symptoms collectively known as Tourette Syndrome, with no clue as to what it was. Tourette's is named after George Gilles de la Tourette, a French neurologist who discovered and classified the disorder in the late 1800's. Tourette's usually starts between age six and 13, and it is genetic, passed on about 3:1, male to female. Conversations with my late father confirmed that both he and his father exhibited symptoms, although neither of them had ever experienced head trauma. However, I believe that either way, my symptoms would have showed up sooner or later.

Tourette's is developmental, not chronic or fatal, meaning it follows you through your life. There is presently no cure, although research is on-going all over the world. Available medication provides some relief, but often with undesirable side-effects. I took Ritalin in fourth grade for a brief period, but it was relatively ineffective in controlling the involuntary movements and sounds. For a month during my senior year in high school, I tried Mellaril, which worked *too* well, requiring great effort on my part to even leave the bed.

A one-week trial in college with Haldol and its lethargic, cotton-mouth inducing side-effects led me to abandon medication, preferring instead the hyper-energetic state and mental gyrations that fueled my drumming. As it turns out, drumming was the best medicine of all for me.

After the bicycle accident and during the very frustrating diagnostic gap, an abundance of misinformation and psychological stress followed. The endless teasing by other kids compounded matters greatly, offering little to build up my shattered self-esteem. Experiencing this uninvited harassment created emotional pain that was bone-deep. I had no control or any indication as to when the "tics" would occur, and it was the disorder's hardest aspect to handle.

One afternoon while playing tag football in Pease Park, shortly after the symptoms had begun, I recall a kid asking me, "Why are you *doing* that stuff?"

I told him with great frustration that I had no idea. As anyone with Tourette's can attest, moments like those never leave you.

/   /

In the early 1960's, proper and correct Tourette's diagnosis was rare; I did not receive mine until I was 20, in 1979. I was repeatedly misdiagnosed wherever my parents took me. It was more than any of us could handle, and during those years, the stress never let up. It took fourteen years to receive a proper diagnosis, during which time I had only one anchor to hold me steadfast in my confused world: music.

The first instrument I can recall laying my hands on was the upright piano in kindergarten. Many people with Tourette's have very strong tactile memories, and I can still, nearly five decades later, vaguely recall the sensation of the ivory keys under my finger tips. What captivated me most were the vibrations that filled me from fingers to head to toes.

This was a year before the symptoms began, so I suppose the musical sensitivity was in place from the start. I can remember resting my head against the school piano keyboard's edge and pressing the keys, immersing myself deeply into the vibrations created by the internal felt hammers striking the tautly drawn steel piano wires. It was an added pleasure and fascination to hold down the sustain foot pedal, which caused the pleasing vibrations to extend as they slowly faded into an acoustical haze.

Tourette's would soon begin to manifest itself strongly, so, any sort of positive diversion was greatly welcomed. Likewise, any hope I had of being a normal kid went out the window every time I jerked my neck or made a strange face or noise. Not knowing the exact cause of the involuntary jerking and grimaces produced a never-ending state of anxiety and frustration, both for myself and my family.

But things were far from lost.

/ /

Music formally entered my world at age six, not long after the first symptoms began. I started taking guitar lessons, and I also had an intriguing interest in percussion. The acoustic guitar was something I became familiar with thanks to the Beatles' arrival in the U.S. that rocked the Western world.

Their success generated a cartoon series I watched faithfully on Saturday mornings, and more than anything, I wanted to learn how to play the guitar. My mother and father had separated, and times were somewhat tough, but my mother found a way to buy me a small brown Harmony acoustic guitar and pay for some lessons. I was ecstatic!

I found relaxation from strumming and plucking the guitar, and that's where I discovered my second attraction to vibration. Sometimes I would place my left ear against the body of the guitar and just close my eyes, diving deep into the resonating tones of a single string or of simple chords. It was soothing, like the piano tones, and it always created a very magical escape.

Another source of simple pleasure was to strike a steel tuning fork and move it back and forth near my ears. In the days before electronic tuning devices, all you had were tuning forks, designed to be struck on a surface to vibrate the tone for an "A" note. You'd tune your "A" string on the guitar from that, and then you'd tune the other strings in relation to it. I loved to place the tuning fork's pronged handle on the guitar's sound board, rest my ear against the body or sometimes the neck, and soak in the resonance.

For brief moments, my involuntary movements ceased when I played the guitar or experimented with the tuning fork. I also found it very easy to tell if another string was out of tune, because I could *feel* the intonation, not just hear it. For a six-year-old kid, this was neat stuff!

Lessons consisted of a weekly ride to the music store, but they didn't last long. I was too distracted, just couldn't concentrate, and the steel guitar strings eventually hurt my fingers. Many people with Tourette's have a very sensitive sense of touch, a strong tactile ability. I should have played a guitar with nylon strings instead, as they are much softer.

The lessons eventually came to an end, but I still looked at my faithful Mel Bay guitar book from time to time to copy the photographed hand positions and try to make guitar chords. And, my maternal grandmother had an acoustic guitar, which I really looked forward to playing when we'd make the road trip north to her home in Fort Worth, Texas. When she passed away, my dad gave me that 1930's Slingerland "Songster" guitar, which I now cherish and still play. It always reminds me of someone who loved to share her love of music.

/ /

Around the end of first grade, the neck jerking and the body spasms were compounded by kids mispronouncing my last name as "Ostrich" instead of Aldridge, and this was every bit as painful as the mimicking of my nervous movements. It was both ironic and appropriate, because I really *was* trying to bury my head in the sand the way that namesake bird does, as much to get away from it all as to find some answers to the never ending questions:

Why was my body doing this? Why couldn't I stop it?
What could I do about it? Would this ever go away?

Tourette Syndrome and Music

Sports were a big part of growing up as a kid in Texas, but they were never something I performed well. Much as I tried, my attention deficit usually made hand-eye concentration a real challenge. Hand-*ear* concentration, however, was another story. It was one with a much more pleasant outcome, starting with some special musical gifts from the Caribbean.

My initial introduction to hand percussion came in the way of native instruments sent by my maternal grandfather from Puerto Rico, to my brother Charlie and I. Two guiros (long, dried, hollowed gourds) and two pairs of maracas (smaller, round gourds filled with seeds, mounted on wooden handles) were objects I greatly enjoyed experimenting with to create sounds through simple motion.

I'd scrape a square, wood-handled, three-pronged wire brush across the serrated gourd's surface, varying the duration of the stroke, zipping back and forth to create brief musical phrases. With the maracas, I'd either swirl them to get a "swooshing" sound, or shake them with tapping motions to get more of an articulated, staccato sound. The maracas' textural aspect, a smooth and polished round wooden surface painted with Caribbean beach scenery, was also pleasant to the touch. This really did enhance the playing experience for me.

I really enjoyed experimenting with the guiro and the maracas, making up my own music and sometimes playing along to records. Doing so helped close the gap between myself and my surroundings. Having not yet received a diagnosis for Tourette's, I felt (and likely also created) a lot of distance between the external world and my own inner anguish. Actually, that distance was my emotional defense, my attempt to flee both the teasing of school kids as well as the disorder whenever and wherever I could.

Surrendering to the sensations of music exploration, immersing myself in it, creating with and making it my own, all became very good things indeed. In those safe moments, I could be a little less removed from the world I'd come to view with great distrust and apprehension, because when you don't know what's coming next, you tend to pull in close and hold on tight. It was nice to be able to relax the grip now and then.

Around that time, I also obtained a wooden tambourine. It too possessed fascinating vibration possibilities of a very soothing nature. It felt good to drum my fingers against the sandpaper-like white drum head, and I liked striking the palm of my hand against the wooden rim. The multiple pairs of metal jingles rattled freely when I rapidly twisted the tambourine back and forth with one hand, and this twisting movement built a strong foundation for future drum stick manipulation.

One of the most interesting and intense exposures to vibrations came from the trains that thundered over the railroad tracks a few hundred yards behind our house, up on a small hill. I can recall many nights falling asleep to the soothing, rolling vibrations of the diesel engines, pulling tons of freight cars from points south to north and back. There was a definite rhythm to the train's movement, and I loved feeling and listening to it. Believe it or not, that sound really helped me connect to very deep aspects of motion, more than I realized at the time, but to a level I would come to understand much later in my life. I think it's safe to say that these instruments and initial elements laid foundation for developing my sensitivity and awareness of vibration, which ultimately led to exploring the relaxing and creative outlet benefits of music.

/   /

My first formal music activities in school came from Casis Elementary, in Austin, where we listened to records and sang along. It was a lot of fun, and in one case I remember, maybe a little too much so. I liked to experiment with sounds by singing in different voices (which I was good at), and one such experiment landed me in what at the time was considered big trouble: no recess. We had to sing along to a Bavarian classic tune called "The Happy Wanderer," and the day the teacher played the German version, I couldn't stop laughing.

Then I began singing the lyrics like a howling dog.

Looking back, the teacher and my friends must have truly thought I was completely out of my mind, but at the time, that song and my interpretation of it was the funniest music I'd ever heard. And as far as dogs went, my voice was actually fairly passable...

In truth, the frustration created by a disorder with no name and no signs of stopping was the sort of experience that drove me into frequent isolation. This withdrawal from the world only intensified when a neighbor down the street gave me his collection of over six-hundred comic books, and I dove headfirst into that colorful fantasy world to further escape the ragged emotional reality of my circumstances.

Between the comics and a small white AM transistor radio I owned, the cartoon images and music soon became my collective safe house, providing escape from the pain and anguish brought on by not knowing what kept tapping on my shoulder and then disappearing when I'd turn 'round and 'round looking for it.

I carried that little radio with me everywhere in the summer of 1966 and often slept with it, falling asleep to songs created without the help of computers and synthesizers. The pop music of the 60's was the real deal, and you could feel the honest energy of the players flowing across the airwaves. It pumped through that little 3-inch speaker without compromise, and I would place the radio against my ear and drink in the rhythm and harmony, connecting and escaping very deeply.

/ /

I reacted physically to certain harmonies, often getting tingles and chills all over my body. The heightened physical sensitivity experienced by many people with Tourette's lends itself to the inherent pleasant benefits and effects of certain music. Today, the advent of digital music players provides similar sensations, plus access to a huge range of songs for relaxing listening pleasure, something I encourage parents to consider for their kids as a source of affordable relief.

Another aspect of my discovering music involved dance. My mom used to teach my brother and I how to waltz, do a square box-step pattern, and other simple moves. As a dancer, I was basically a bust, but what I discovered from my mom's best intentions was that I loved listening to music and the physical/emotional reaction it produced in me... even if I did have two left feet.

It's ironic that one of the artists my mom listened to was Julius Wechter, leader of the Baja Marimba Band. Ironic because I came to California to meet him when I was 20, after having finally received an accurate diagnosis of Tourette's. Julius Wechter also had Tourette Syndrome, and we'll talk a lot more about him in Chapter 12.

Along with the Baja Marimba Band, I often listened to music by Herb Alpert and the Tijuana Brass. Alpert's drummer, Nick Ceroli, was a solid timekeeper, and as with the irony of listening to Julius Wechter, I would meet Nick many years later in Los Angeles.

I also liked the vocal harmonies of The Mamas and the Papas, especially "California Dreamin'," with its minor chord structure that resonated from head to toe. Simon and Garfunkel's music had a similar effect, particularly "Like A Bridge Over Trouble Water." An appropriate title, considering how far away it took me from whatever my body was doing at the time. These groups, along with the Beatles, formed my musical foundation. They may seem ancient now, but their artistry is timeless.

I listened to their vinyl records on a faded green, fold-out portable Zenith stereo that became one of my best musical friends. That little record player stayed with me all the way out to California in my early twenties, and it too played a big part in my musical development, because it allowed me to play along with records and develop my musician's ear. With that stereo and my little white transistor AM radio, I had two great musical friends and a way to escape a very unwanted (and at the time, unnamed) Tourette visitor.

At least for a little while.

Chapter 2

Meeting Drumming Magic

The drum set initially found its way into my world after watching The Beatles' cartoon series during the early 1960's. Along with wanting to be a guitar player, whenever a song would come on in our classic Rambler, I would wail away on the car dashboard or the back seat, trying to copy drummer Ringo Starr's pulsing beats and energy.

To my mother's credit, she rarely turned down the volume, recognizing the tremendous happiness and release being experienced by her extremely hyperactive son. To my brother Charlie's credit, he never tried to tie my hands behind my back to get some peace and quiet.

They were both *incredibly* patient and accommodating.

A moment that remains clearly painted into my memory was the first time I saw a *real* drum set. I was enrolled in weekly tennis lessons at the Austin Athletic Club, and as with most of my sports efforts, the lessons yielded more frustration than anything else. One day, there was a live band performing inside, and a red sparkle drum set in the gymnasium was being played by a kid whose percussive power filled the room with a level of intensity I'd never experienced or imagined.

The ringing of the cymbals to a simple rock beat, the thundering bass drum, the crack of the snare drum; these were sounds I'd *never* forget. They were beckoning calls to a door

I'd eventually walk through, and it's that walk I credit with giving me so much control over my nervous condition. As I stood there listening to the wall of sounds filling the room, all I could think was, "I want to be able to do *that*."

Music was never the same after that day. I began listening to drums even more intently, trying to understand what was really happening. I soon learned to mimic "Wipe Out," a top-40 hit by The Safaris. Their drummer, Ron Wilson, set a drum solo standard that has remained a classic for over forty-five years.

The cool thing was, I could actually play it with one hand, which turned lunchroom tables and park recreation storage bins into fair percussion game. My hand drumming earned curious attention and approval from fellow second graders, who would eagerly place their ears against the surfaces to hear my rapid-fire two fingered attacks. I would alternate my thumb and middle finger with a wrist-twisting movement, similar to what I had experimented with on my tambourine. The significance revealed itself years later when it assisted my development of very fast drumstick manipulation.

My odd drumming ability seemed to earn an additional level of acceptance (and in a way, some self-acceptance) that I definitely liked. This became my first positive taste of socialization, all brought on by simply letting my body tap into Tourette's and let it speak through rhythm. Kids never made fun of my raw drumming effort. In fact, they encouraged it, and this in turn drew me closer to the group. Go figure...

Tourette Syndrome and Music

But any acceptance was welcomed, and it stoked my inner fires to become very good at whatever yielded those results. I was clumsy at sports, but music was clearly a ride I was wired for. My disability was gradually becoming an ability; however, it still remained an ever-present intrusion, with no signs of improving.

/ /

It wouldn't be until my family moved to Charlottesville, Virginia, a few years later, that I got my hands on an actual pair of drum sticks, and it was there that I was exposed to one final foundation instrument that helped me develop my musical ear and be able to play just about anything I heard.

It was a bright, canary-yellow plastic recorder, a flute-like instrument that we played in fourth grade music classes at McIntire Elementary. The recorder had a limited range of notes, but I enjoyed experimenting with them, creating and improvising over many songs. The connectivity between musical thought and expression is what's important here, as it was my first development of a flow of creative consciousness.

The best memory I have of my recorder was playing along to the Beatles song "Fool On The Hill," from the Beatles' *Magical Mystery Tour* album. A neighbor in Austin had given me a copy, and I listened to it every chance I got. I couldn't focus well enough to read music, but I could play "Fool On The Hill" by ear, and that was a life-changing experience. I didn't know *how* I was able to do it, I just knew that I *could* do it… and for a nine-year-old, that was awesome!

This bit of musical magic established a fascinating and relaxing connection between my mind and body. It was almost like I was singing the flute sounds in my mind, and out they would come, *exactly* the way I wanted them to. This connection grew stronger with time, as we'll be discovering shortly. Musical moments like these add amazing color to your world, and in my case, they certainly provided respite and escape from the never-ending and never-wanted movements.

/ . /

During this period of my life in fourth grade, I was prescribed Ritalin to hopefully calm what had been yet again misdiagnosed as simple hyperactivity. My movements and nervousness had progressed to my throat and mouth, causing me to stammer and obsess on certain hard syllables like the letter "b." The stomach contractions had gotten worse, and my obsessive/compulsive actions had increased as well, such as having to touch a glass to my top lip and then my bottom lip before being able to drink from it.

Socially, I was getting along better, and I was playing football and baseball well enough, yet still usually being chosen towards the end of the roster. Little things like this didn't make interacting easier, but I was still able to have some fun, and, thankfully, no one in Virginia *ever* thought to mispronounce my name as "Ostrich." Three years of *that* agonizing verbal bullying back in Austin had left me wishing I could have legally changed my last name to Smith.

I also had a crush on a pretty girl named Rose whom I finally got up the nerve to talk to on the very last day of school. Turns out she liked me, and had for some time. I learned something valuable from that experience: Tourette's can make you afraid and cause you to delay reaching out to see what's there and what you can do… if you let it.

But if you *do* reach out, you just might be very pleasantly surprised by who and what you find.

Tourette Syndrome and Music

Chapter 3

The Coveted Seat

I was formally introduced to the drum set under the tutelage of Ken Berry, my fourth grade music teacher's son. My mom enrolled me in snare drum studies with Ken after I became inspired watching an older student play a marching snare drum on the school playground during a May Day ceremony. I was mesmerized as the drummer executed a flawless roll, where the sticks vibrated in alternating double-strokes so quickly and smoothly that I literally could not see the tips beyond a blur.

It was pure sonic magic.

The memory of my first drumming lesson remains sharp. I arrived at Ken's house and was treated to thirty minutes on my feet in front of a snare drum mounted on a stand, where I clumsily attempted to hold the sticks while repeating beats that Ken instructed me to play.

The first steps were simple single strokes; I tapped the snare drum head again and again with the same hand, then switched hands. Next, Ken had me alternate left/right, left/right.

Finally, he had me tap twice with each hand, over and over. This exercise prepared me to play a drum roll, the rapid meshing of left-left/right-right strokes that created an uninterrupted flowing sound. And with that, the drumming doors swung *wide* open...

These fundamental elements were crucial building blocks for further hand development. They were also exciting, because they immediately enabled me to play a drum sound I was hearing in my head. During that first lesson, I asked Ken if I could just "play something," a simple march beat I'd heard somewhere. He didn't mind, and his approval helped me tap into all the creative drumming that has followed since, because the humble stages of being able to express inner sounds and thoughts were suddenly at my fingertips.

I couldn't articulate the sounds exactly, but this didn't matter nearly as much as that I had discovered a vehicle for expression. I could hear the sounds in my head (a process called *audiation*), and I could feel the muscles in my fingers and wrists wanting to move like they already knew what to do. I could also hear the replaying of the simple snare drum marching cadence in my mind.

Okay, now *this* was cool!

The snare drum cadence repeated itself with no effort from myself, a phenomenon that I would later discover was related to *palilalia* (the involuntary repeating of one's own words). This component of Tourette's, along with *echolalia* (the urge to repeat other peoples' words), definitely helped further transform the disability into a musical ability.

This "replaying" process seemed to send muscle impulses to my fingers that in some way assured me I could indeed play what I was hearing. I have consistently experienced this sensation since that time in varying degrees. If I heard a drumming thought, or sang it out loud, I could *will* it to happen, and the appropriate muscle action followed. Put another way: if I could *hear* it, I could *play* it, and this became (and remains) a very important means for me to use in exploring any musical instrument.

/ /

Physical sensations imbed deeply in my memory, and I can still feel the imprint of Ken Berry's drumming the first time he sat down behind the drum set and played for me. Overhead white tract lighting poured down on his body as he moved all four limbs at once in a blisteringly elaborate sonic dance. The tonal combinations of cymbals and drums blended into an overwhelming mix of percussive dizziness.

By the time Ken was about a quarter the way through his demonstration, my head was spinning. How could anyone's hands and feet move so fast, with such control and deliberate action? When Ken finished his boggling display, he let me sit down behind the drums, taking the coveted seat.

I can still recall the heat from the overhead tract lights, much like stage spotlights I'd know in years to come. My legs barely reached the pedals to my left and right that drove the hi-hat and bass drum, and my arms had to stretch slightly to reach the drums and cymbals. It felt quite surreal.

Now the thing is, when you sit down behind a drum set for the very first time, you literally do not know what to do with yourself. First you tap surfaces to hear what sounds are produced. Next, you stretch and extend your legs to press the bass drum pedal beater into the bass drum head, and its impact resonates through your body.

Then, you awkwardly step on the hi-hat pedal to compress its two cymbals shut, creating a "chick" sound. You generally tap them with your dominant hand to hear the sound of them closed, and from there, you might try to formulate a parcel of a beat you can recall from a song. Or, you may resort to a simple "boom" of the right foot on the bass drum and then a "tap" of the left hand on the snare drum.

Boom, tap, boom, tap, boom, tap...

Adding a cymbal to create a timekeeping pulse often throws the whole concentration mix upside down, as the coordination to execute the combination is usually a big challenge. It's much later that you learn how to *hear sounds together*, knowing both what to listen for and how the associated sensation should feel in your head and throughout your body.

/ /

From that first lesson, I found an amazing and unbelievable place where I could escape the anguish of Tourette's and become lost in uninhibited movement and exploration. The release from stress and anxiety was immediate. By allowing me to do whatever I wanted, Ken Berry let my case of Tourette's breathe, and for the first time ever, be a *good* thing.

Tourette Syndrome and Music

That opportunity was my most intense experience to date with a socially acceptable form of movement, one that was free of censure and ridicule. However, it was really kind of a tease, because we lived in an apartment, and the only way I could practice my drumming lessons was to hit pillows and use the lid of my mother's sewing kit to create a poor man's ride cymbal.

I would play along to the Beatles' *Magical Mystery Tour* and *Yellow Submarine* albums, denting the sewing kit lid as I wore the tracks down while pounding the stuffing out of my pillow drum set. I don't think a day ever passed during that time that I didn't long for a set of drums almost as much as I longed for answers as to what was causing my body to move uncontrollably. I had high hopes for both and never gave up on either one.

So believe me, no matter how bad your tics are, it's a blessing to at least know *what* to call them. It lets you move forward into your future without having to constantly search your past for clues. At the age of nine, I would have given anything for that, but at least there was more cool drumming to come, as I would discover when we moved north a year later, to Newark, Delaware.

Chapter 4

Continuing Education

They call Delaware the Diamond State, a nickname given by Thomas Jefferson, supposedly because of its location along the Eastern seaboard. For me, it was a place where my drumming education would continue, expanding well beyond anywhere I thought it could ever go.

During my first year in Newark, I was in the Gallaher Elementary School band, where I mostly played snare drum (and once, even a live drum set) in the symphonic band. I was also rehearsing with the Blue Rock Drum and Bugle Corps, located a few miles north, in Wilmington. The positive aspects of these endeavors provided me with both improved drumming ability and a greater sense of group involvement and acceptance.

The curious looks on kids' faces never quite went away, although being able to move and make sounds with drum sticks did help mask the involuntary movements and noises I was making. That was the great thing about being a young drummer: people *expected* you to be hyper and restless!

So, I would sing and tap out beats in many situations, like classrooms, lunchrooms, schoolyards and playgrounds, finding that less negative attention was paid to me as a result. Drumming became a perfect cloak to hide behind, and it helped me buy time to figure out why I could not sit still.

Tourette Syndrome and Music

By now (fifth grade), my verbal tics had shown few signs of decreasing, and the physical tics continued to migrate unpredictably from one part of my body to another, as if they were somehow actual living entities trapped beneath the skin, looking for a way out, by any means.

Meanwhile, my social reality remained a never ending struggle to find ways to mask my behaviors. It's a full-time job for some people, and I guess I was working about seventy-five percent of the time. Whenever a new set of symptoms showed up, I had to reinvent my coping behaviors and find new ways to become as invisible as possible.

The *good* news was that the elementary school band and the rudimental drum corps helped me develop my hands to a higher degree, which in turn allowed me to better express the ideas I was hearing in my musical mind. This helped me develop even more control and release. Sometimes I'd just let whatever was inside find its way out through my drumming; that's when the most interesting sensations occurred.

These were the roots of sub-conscious flow, a technique that improvisational musicians rely on for their deepest communications. When you can use something like Tourette's to tap into *that*, it really is amazing.

/ /

I did well with both the drum kit and rudimental forms of drumming, much more so in playing than in being able to read sheet music. My reading attention span was barely useful, but I could sit down behind a drum set and play freely for hours. However, it would still be a couple of years before I actually received my own drum set.

So, in the meantime, I pounded away on my trusty Remo practice pad with my Regal Tip drum sticks. I truly loved the lacquered feel of those sticks in my anxious hands. The round practice pad had a small drum head attached under a frame device, and I spent many hours using it to work on the basic drumming rudiments I was learning through the Blue Rock Drum and Bugle Corps.

I really owe the foundation of my hand ability to them, even though my involvement was somewhat brief. Rudimental drumming finds its origins in military field drumming dating back to the Revolutionary War. The patterns also helped drummers develop technique and stick control. In my case, they gave me greater focus and direction for the tremendous amounts of energy that raged endlessly and demanded release.

It felt great to make the sticks bounce and have a form of movement that was socially acceptable. But while the drum corps involvement was helpful to my hand development, it soon lost its appeal, due to the boredom of just smacking drumsticks on planks of wood in a room filled with other young drummers learning the twenty-six traditional rudiments. These practice sessions simply lacked the excitement and immediate gratification I craved and was able to obtain by sitting behind the drum set. Believe me, *that* experience was second to none.

Tourette Syndrome and Music

I recall very clearly my first live drum set performance, when I played the theme from the television series "Hogan's Heroes" with the Gallaher Elementary School band. I was joined by another drummer (Ronnie Cox) on a second drum set, and what made the experience unique was that Ronnie also had a disability, one requiring him to wear a leg brace. I suppose the odds are extraordinarily high that my first actual live drum set performance would be a duet with someone who also lived with (and overcame) a disability!

The positive benefit of interacting with other musicians and of receiving applause and acceptance from other kids was my first real dose of public music therapy. Granted, the theme from "Hogan's Heroes" was a cheesy song, but the audience was intrigued by the idea of hearing and seeing two drummers play it, and they shared their applause with enthusiasm. The only thing cooler would have been to be in the *other* drum duo, where those guys got to the play the theme from "Hawaii Five-0." Those drum fills were awesome!

Regardless, the very thing that caused my body to move involuntarily was now serving me in ways I could never have imagined, allowing the nervous movements to become streamlined into a single performance purpose with boundless energy. My battered self-esteem never rose so high as after playing a song and being allowed to just be myself. The applause was nice too!

These experiences were addicting, but in some ways, not so good. Coupled with how Tourette's both energized and enabled my limbs to play with furious intensity, I eventually spent more of my early drumming years showing off than actually playing musically. The need for acceptance overrode the call for restrained musical performance, and it definitely would've been helpful to have received more guidance in this area. However, I was not very mature at the time, and I would have likely ignored that guidance and just played whatever I wanted to anyway. It would be awhile before I settled down and began to really become a musician.

/ /

My mother eventually purchased a chrome snare drum for me to practice my rudiments on, but, we lived in an apartment. This meant that before being allowed to play, I had to ask permission of *all* the neighbors first, and then lay a towel over the drum to further mute it. Taking a shower with your clothes on accurately describes what it felt like to not be able to experience the full vibrational range of my snare drum.

I was glued to the radio and the top-40 hits that poured out at the time, and I had just discovered Led Zeppelin, Black Sabbath, and The Who, courtesy of some older kids in the neighborhood. The drummers in these groups were incredible power-hitters and artists in their own right.

John Bonham's solid, bombastic beats and beautiful cymbal work for Led Zeppelin imprinted a sense of artistry in me to not just hit the drums, but to play them with deep, heartfelt feeling. Bill Ward's blistering fills for Black Sabbath brought unmistakable jazz-schooled hands to the world of heavy metal and showed me how to bridge that gap. Keith Moon, iconic drummer for The Who, re-wrote much of rock drumming's book with his over-the-top drum fills and compositional style.

I borrowed a little from each of these three pioneering greats, enjoying their unbridled approach to the drums. They hit hard and fast, with nothing held back, and if I needed permission to explore the power of rhythm, these guys granted it by virtue of their exploding performances.

Another group I listened to a lot was Steppenwolf. Their now legendary hit, "Born to be Wild," was filled with powerful drumming by Jerry Edmonton and his classic killer drum fill in the middle that blasted out of the speakers. I could not play that song enough. Heavy metal thunder indeed!

It became the biker world's anthem of sorts when it was featured in the movie, "*Easy Rider*." It's ironic that I loved this song so much, because about twenty years later, I ended up writing full-time for *Easyriders*, the world's largest motorcycle lifestyle magazine.

Rounding out my early drumming influences, Iron Butterfly's "In-A-Gadda-Da-Vida" was also a huge hit at the time, featuring an extended drum solo unlike anything ever heard before on pop radio. Ron Bushy influenced generations of drummers with his psychedelic era-defining improvisation, adding colorful new meaning to the classic phrase, "Give the drummer some."

Tourette Syndrome and Music

The drum corps experience had helped me refine my hands enough to copy a lot of what I heard on many records, and I committed that particular solo to memory, pounding it out on different pillows in my bedroom until I was too tired to go on. While my drumming was improving, my social life wasn't doing too badly either. I seemed to be able to make kids laugh, so, I became something of a class clown. As long as the laughter was with me and not at me, I could live with it.

But the truth was, my clowning around really was disruptive to the teachers' attempts at imparting some proper schooling to a group of wild ones. During one intense correctional visit to the principal's office, Mr. Sharkey sat me down and made something very clear: the other kids *were* laughing at me, not with me.

To his credit and wisdom, this graying principal knew something was wrong with me, and he knew I didn't know what it was. Mr. Sharkey's compassion gave me great insight into how to see a situation for more than what it appeared to be. A very valuable life lesson indeed. I shaped up pretty quickly after that visit.

/ /

Sports remained a lukewarm pursuit, and school continued to be a challenge, especially in subjects requiring concentration. Math was utterly agonizing, and science wasn't much better. English, on the other hand, became a favorite because of the creative writing exercises we were given. Reading six hundred comic books (recall my acquired collection from Austin) filled my head with a great deal of imaginative energy, and it fed my creativity to no end. Writing became yet another escape vehicle, although not quite as powerful as music. Funny thing was, many years later, I would actually make a living by writing for some of the nation's leading music and motorcycle magazines.

The social benefits of music were great, but they were not without some rivalries, and I mention this because around this time, drumming became more competitive than artistic for. This misdirection tended to isolate rather than integrate me with the other kids, and I think it was definitely something I should have avoided.

I felt kind of slighted, though, because I couldn't read as well as the other drummers; but in my mind, my hands and natural ability were forces to be reckoned with. I wanted recognition, which was driven out of insecurity and the need to compensate in some way. Because of this, I craved approval on many levels, which clearly tainted my music performance.

However, when you play for recognition and attention rather than for the music, you rob yourself *and* the art. Of course, these are not things most eleven-year-olds are immediately aware of. And sometimes, receiving attention is not always such a good thing.

I remember only too well hearing an auditorium of kids laughing at me during a spelling bee once in sixth grade. I thought I was doing something they liked, which translated into acceptance and appreciation, and everything seemed great... until later.

We had an after-school bowling league, and usually it was a lot of fun, but on that particular day, kids kept coming up to me and asking, "Why were you making all those weird faces and noises during the spelling bee?"

I learned to spell "h-u-m-i-l-i-a-t-e-d" that afternoon.

Yet despite the nervous spasms and movements during this period, I attracted the attention of two of the prettiest girls in the school. Considering the state of constant fear I walked around in, this seemed completely impossible in the realm of perceived possibilities. What I learned from those experiences was that even if you have something wrong with you, some people can and will look past it to see the *real* you and want to know more about you.

For those with Tourette's reading this, please remember: the kindness within is easily seen by those who have it in themselves, and it's *those* people you'll find you have the most in common with, even if they don't share a neurological disorder.

Because just like you, they are the real deal.

Chapter 5

My Very Own Coveted Chair

Graduating to Ogletown Middle School and attending junior high meant being able to audition for the jazz ensemble. This was quite a step up from the classical music I'd been playing in elementary school, and I remember very well the day I walked nervously (even more so than usual) into the music room and met the band director, Mr. Bernard Kosc.

He reminded me of my dad, with a thick mane of black hair and a very intense look. I wanted to make a good impression, but I couldn't read music worth anything, so I just played with passion instead. It must have been enough, because Mr. Kosc let me join the two other drummers (Fred Layou and Jim Shepherd) in the jazz band.

I loved playing this stuff, and I was *very* grateful that Jim would sit behind me and help point out where I was as I struggled endlessly to read the sheet music. For the first time, I felt like I was really part of a team, and not chosen last on the roster.

Still, attending a new school was always a challenge, and of course, there were the usual round of questions about my behavior. Having no name for the mysterious nervous disorder continued to make my personal life away from music a series of physiological upsets during most every waking moment.

But... it soon got *much* better...

Tourette Syndrome and Music

For years, I'd craved getting my own kit, and finally, on Christmas Day, 1972, my dreams came true. My mother bought me a blue sparkle, 3-piece drum set, which I could not set up fast enough along with my chrome snare drum in the basement of our home.

Finally, a full-blast escape from Tourette's!

I became obsessed with practice and playing, rushing home and then downstairs every day after school into my bedroom to crank up my trusty Zenith fold-out stereo to play along with. I would bang and flail for hours, usually to a state of near exhaustion, with never a complaint from my mom (who ironically taught deaf education). As with banging on the car dashboard and backseat, she saw and encouraged the benefits of release and relief I received from actual drumming.

/ /

The control of my limbs increased with steady practice, and combined with my new involvement in the martial arts, a greater degree of focus and concentration was obtained and put to good use. The twice-weekly karate classes my brother and I were taking also provided a healthy outlet for energy, and they were a perfect environment in which to develop much needed personal discipline and confidence.

Drumming's greatest benefit was the simple permission to explode, as opposed to the constant social requirements to sit still and be silent in most settings. When I played, I held *nothing* back. And while my timekeeping ability was not solid, and the lack of focus and minimal music reading skills remained impediments to progress, the exploration of sounds and unrestricted movements were what brought me the greatest joys. The other skills would improve later... but not without a *great* deal of work.

Pursuing artistic freedom fueled my goal to master the drum set and to be able to emulate my drumming heroes at the time, as well as some new ones I'd discovered. They included Don Brewer (Grand Funk Railroad), Carl Palmer (Emerson, Lake and Palmer), and Buddy Rich, the legendary jazz great. What they all shared was a musical exploration of the drum set that went well beyond mere timekeeping.

Don Brewer played a trademark triplet pattern between his hands and feet that became something of an obsession for me to master. It was fast, powerful, and seriously endorphin-stirring. I *loved* how hard the he hit; just raw, basic, and solid.

The grit of Grand Funk Railroad was music I fell asleep to many a night, and their 1970 *Grand Funk Live Album* made me dream of hearing audiences react to my future drumming. It was the sound of hope to hang on to during the increasingly tension-filled years approaching high school, when my body and its hormones were beginning their inevitable clashes.

And again, in an odd twist of fate, I would grow up to become a professional music magazine writer and actually interview Don Brewer for *DRUM!* magazine. That was one of the real highlights of my professional music journalism life.

Tourette Syndrome and Music

Carl Palmer had hands like lightning, and I was captivated by his use of speed and power. The Tourette mind does not take well to sitting idle and calm, so, hearing drummers with great ability only served to fuel the electrified neurons. I could come close to matching Palmer's energy here and there, and doing so more fully became the ultimate goal.

Palmer had a MASSIVE stainless steel drum set at one time, with multiple tom-toms, two bass drums, and two huge Paiste gongs behind him. He was beyond over-the-top, and he brought a certain distinguished flare and class to rock drumming. I watched his every move on weekend rock concert TV shows, cherishing every second I had to study from such a master.

Many years later, I had the opportunity to meet Palmer and tell him how much his playing had influenced me. It was a meeting I never dreamed I'd have, and I was very honored to share those few minutes with a living rock drumming idol.

But it was Buddy Rich who quickly became my biggest inspiration, a jazz legend who set the standard by which all drummers were measured. His hands made most other guys look like they were sitting still. Rich's drumming stirred waves of euphoria in me, and along with the other drummers mentioned, my working to get close to what he was doing was an endless source of energy and endorphin release.

Buddy Rich's playing also introduced me to the real depths of improvisational freedoms. Jazz was particularly fascinating, in that it mirrored many of the inner workings of Tourette's, and much of my life was unexpected and unpredictable. I had to learn to socially improvise in many situations to mask the symptoms, or, at least hopefully distract people from noticing the movements too much. In a way then, I was living and discovering the essence of jazz just about every waking moment.

Rock drumming was definitely the foundation of my playing up to that point, but discovering jazz greatly expanded my ability to express myself, and it provided a very cerebral outlet for the boundless energy. It was yet another style of music that welcomed me into the family of drumming, connecting me to an entirely new lineage of legendary musicians.

I became very hungry for this newfound way of playing, and I wanted to know as much as I could about it, but to do that, I had to go far beyond just playing songs by ear. It became pretty clear that the time had come for me to get serious, buckle down, and learn how to read better.

So, off to formal drum lessons I went.

Chapter 6

Focus! Focus! Focus!

I should have gotten into lessons when I first received my drum set, but it had been the very *absence* of a teacher that had let me play exactly as I pleased, pounding into the drum heads, smashing the cymbals, and exercising complete freedom of movement in the privacy of my basement. Besides, I was a thirteen-year-old drumming volcano. There *was* no off switch!

This exploration of self-induced music therapy continued for about a year, during which time I honed my raw talent by playing along to my favorite 45's and LP's for hours on my faithful Zenith fold-up stereo. I'd been able to find escape and peace for brief periods of time, but the muscle spasms and tics remained intense. While the vocal tics seemed to die down a little, my now twitching eyebrows certainly made for an attention-getting visual spectacle, which was definitely, absolutely, an unwanted one.

With encouragement from some of the neighborhood drummers, particularly my friend Jim Shepherd, I enrolled in drum set lessons at The Percussion Center, in Newport, Delaware. Dick Kenny's teaching staff were patient and encouraging, realizing that the future of drumming was always in the next crop of students. Mr. Kenny taught me how to read much better and to approach the drum set like a pro, but even more importantly, he introduced me to four-way coordination, the playing of different beats with different limbs at the same time. THIS re-wired my brain forever!

It's actually something of a sound illusion, and the man who wrote *the* book on this concept was the late Jim Chapin. He was and remains a legend in the drumming world for his work with four-way coordination, and I was extremely fortunate to have taken a few lessons from him through the Percussion Center during his monthly visits down from New York City.

When Chapin wrote his classic instructional text, "Advanced Techniques for the Modern Drummer," in 1948, he turned the drumming world upside down with the idea that you could keep a beat with one hand and create independent rhythm patterns separately with the other, while also using your feet to play the bass drum and hi-hat cymbals. Prior to his publication, no one had articulated or demonstrated teaching concepts in a such a formalized manner.

Chapin's limb independence concepts gave me the tools to develop tremendous control over my body, unlike any I'd had before or could have even imagined. The exercises also helped me become much more aware of my muscles and nerves, and of the connection between my mind and body.

Now, instead of wanting to escape the muscle tics, I dove in head-first and went straight to the source, to make my limbs do *exactly* what I wanted them to do. It was a real challenge to master the basics of four-limb coordination, but once I did, I was able to incorporate them into my jazz drumming and become a much more musical player. I developed greater control over my volume as well, paying better attention to dynamic levels, not just blasting the drums with all I had.

This discipline, coupled with what I'd learned in the martial arts, gave me powerful tools with which to better handle Tourette's. It didn't make the disorder go away, but it didn't make me want to run away from it as much either. I gained greater mental and physical control, which I then took to broader and stronger levels in many styles of music.

Joe Brancato was another teacher at the school, and he had amazing hands. Joe liked that I had fast hands and feet, and he encouraged me to develop those abilities to their fullest. I remember him telling me once that it was all right to be a "gunslinger," saying that it was okay to be competitive.

I believed this at the time, but looking back, I realize that I took Joe's advice a bit too far and became less musical and more bombastic in my playing sometimes. A drummer is a musician first and foremost, but is also someone who can easily overpower most other acoustic instruments. What I eventually learned over many years was that there has to be a balance of musicality, expression, and artistic responsibility with whatever instrument you play.

That fact cannot and must not be ignored.

/ /

Mr. Kenny and Joe Brancato built the foundations of my jazz drumming, which dramatically improved my overall playing ability and confidence. As a result, I felt so positive that I eventually approached my junior high music teacher, Mrs. Betty Moudy, about putting on a drum set demonstration for our music class. I had accumulated a large kit by this time, with multiple drums and cymbals, and I wanted to present the drum set as a valid musical instrument, not just as an oversized metronome.

Mrs. Moudy welcomed the enthusiasm for music she'd encouraged in us, and my initial presentation of limb flailing and semi-organized bashing was expanded with her further urging me to present the demonstration in the middle school auditorium for several other classes. Now *that* was fun!

I explained how the drums were not only designed to keep time, but could also be played as a solo improvisational instrument. The audience obviously could not hear the music in my head (some tunes by Grand Funk Railroad I'd memorized), but I followed the inner music faithfully and unleashed my drumming ability accordingly.

The kids and teachers probably didn't know what to make of the day; they most likely enjoyed being out of the stuffy classroom more than anything else. But it was a day that I made the most of, shoring up frazzled nerves and self-esteem, thanks to a wonderful music educator who was deeply dedicated to encouragement of the arts.

I do owe so very much to Mrs. Moudy for providing that rare opportunity. I think it's one of the reason I now enjoy giving drum set/drum circle demos, because they often remind of those first live performances, where I was playing solo, just being and discovering the real me and my inner artist.

/ /

As my reading gradually improved, my appreciation of the drum set's sound possibilities expanded as well. Discovering King Crimson's *Court of the Crimson King* introduced me to the masterful drumming of Michael Giles. His playing on that legendary progressive rock album took my thinking about drums and cymbals to an almost mystical level.

This was particularly true of cymbals. The delicate tonalities produced by a light touch on them were a source of great pleasure during practice and performances. The thick, grooved ride cymbal served as a primary timekeeping surface when tapped with drum stick, producing a "pinging" sound to articulate the tempo. Its thick center bell would ring out with distinct pitch, and the edges (struck with the side of a drumstick) generated a darker, well-defined tone.

The thinner crash cymbals, when played with felt-tipped mallets, created a shimmering and rapidly evolving gong-like ring. Drawing wire brushes across either the ride or crash cymbals produced faint wisps of ringing. My favorite cymbal of all was (and remains) the China-type, with its flanged uprising edge that unleashed the raw beauty of pure metal explosion. Of all the cymbal types I've ever played, nothing gets me out of me like a vintage 1970's 22" Zildjian China.

Combinations of sticks, mallets, and brushes on the cymbals and drums provided rewarding musical experiments when I closed my eyes and moved my hands to discover what sorts of sounds would arise. Part of the pleasure in letting go was seeing (or hearing, I suppose) what would happen, an event of great therapeutic benefit. I *never* tired of that discovery dance, and the more I worked on it, the more my focus towards expressing myself improved.

/ /

I'd like to close out the middle school years by telling you about the performance our jazz band gave on the last day of school, because for me, it was nothing short of awesome. We'd been practicing for this show for months, and it was the first time I'd had a chance to play the drums alone in a band in public. Now it was time to deliver.

We had stage lights basking down on us in the auditorium, and I thought about the heat from the tract lighting at Ken Berry's house, my first drum teacher. I think and hope he'd have been proud of my pushing past an ever-present and huge unknown to make sure the show went on. The energy radiating from the audience was another form of heat, and in the coming years, I craved that connection and approval, because it filled a cavernous confidence void.

As I candidly shared in the Introduction, Tourette's can often leave you in a constant state of fear and uncertainty, enough to paralyze you at times. But oddly, the only fear I felt the day of our performance was hoping I didn't drop my drum sticks! Mr. Kosc, our band director, helped keep us focused, and he channeled our performances to bring out the best in us. Filling the auditorium with music filled our souls with music, and it was one of the best days of my life.

I definitely wanted more of *this*.

Tourette Syndrome and Music

Chapter 7

Percussive Explorations

I entered high school in 1973, and my musical growth advanced with exposure to more challenging jazz and its very gifted family of drummers, thanks to the inspiring tutelage of Glasgow High School's first band director, L. Jerome Rehberg. I'll be forever grateful for this experience, because as is worth repeating, the unexpected nature of jazz closely mirrored my body's own improvised and unexpected compositions.

Mr. Rehberg's support gave me tremendous confidence with which to proceed both musically and socially. Equally important, Mr. Rehberg's focus on teamwork aided greatly in preventing me from remaining isolated. *This* I needed.

I played in the jazz, marching, and symphonic bands for four years, gaining positive experiences which helped ease the teasing and ridicule that had thankfully reduced somewhat in part due to the increased control I had over my body through drumming. I refined this control aspect during practice sessions by closing my eyes and feeling all the muscles involved with executing a particular rhythm pattern.

Doing this allowed me to become highly sensitized to the nerve endings around my fingers and the tendons in my ankles. I'd always had a very sensitive sense of touch, and it served drumming well when it came to developing the balance of the sticks in my hand and the distribution of weight on my feet.

This focus led me to think more in terms of movement than in terms of creating a sound. I paid much closer attention to the feeling (the physical and mental sensation) than the actual production of a tone, an emphasis that initially inhibited developing my musicality. I clearly should have given more attention to this instead of always trying to be a soloing attention seeker. But I forged ahead, blissfully ignorant at the time, wanting to master whatever it took to make my hands and feet as fast and loud as possible. How else could I recreate, express, and attempt to manage the raging storms within?

/ . /

Fortunately, an unexpected balance was found, one that brought a heightened sense of self-awareness and expressive ability that helped counter the emphasis on the physical. It was a very significant experience, one that took my musicality to a much higher level.

One day during a solo practice session while replaying a song in my head, I somehow became able to manipulate the musical instruments I was hearing and improvise with their sound. I not only heard music in my mind; I was *creating* the sounds of the instruments in my mind, actually composing and thinking in musical terms, the same way I did with words.

This was very cool!

It was like having a conversation between several musical instruments, and I was doing all the talking. This process is called *audiation*. Pretty soon, I was able to mentally mimic and manipulate any instrument, changing the pitch, tempo, and just about any other sound quality I desired. The waves of rhythmic ideas flowing as a stream of consciousness into my hands and feet now had musical accompaniment that I could create and control.

Awesome!

From these elating practice sessions, I developed a more thematic sense of music, where drum fills became a voice similar to a saxophone or trumpet being improvised over a chord structure sustained by the "band" in my head. I was literally thinking in terms of multiple musical instruments and their sounds. It was the most amazing thing I'd ever experienced, and from there, my musical growth really took off with a creative roar.

In the movie *Amadeus*, about the life of composer/pianist Wolfgang Amadeus Mozart, the lead actor discusses being able to compose in his head. I cannot emphasize how much this process changed my musical life, as it was yet another way to control some aspects of my thinking.

With Tourette's, your mind is constantly bouncing you off the walls of your own head, exploding in all directions like a bag of fireworks thrown onto a bonfire. And the thoughts don't just go; they take you with them as you beg them to please, please, please SLOW DOWN! But they do not, and you often have little choice but to be dragged along for the bumpy neurotransmitter ride.

So, when I discovered that I could actually get some sort of grip on things by creating musical instrument sounds in my mind, you can be sure it changed everything.

And *much* for the better.

/ /

Teen hormones had now fully coupled with the never-ending physical stress of Tourette's, and they demanded a very intense outlet. To that end, the drum set also became a source of physical exercise. Meanwhile, my mental processes raced ahead of what tried to pass as concentration, with urges to move my hands and feet as fast and furiously as possible.

My reading was so-so, and it seemed futile to work on the traditional timekeeping role that most drummers followed, because my urges to release tension were never-ending. Instead, I spent hours studying my drumming idols' soloing capabilities, desperately wanting to be able to move that fast.

The most significant turning point in this pursuit came during the summer of 1974, at our school band camp. Ken Rosenberg, a well-respected local high school drummer, showed me an exercise when I was fourteen that greatly increased the speed and movement efficiency of my hands:

R L L R R L: a repeated triplet pattern, counted 1-2-3-4-5-6

(R = right hand, L = left hand)

Imagine your drumming hands moving slowly, then gradually increasing in tempo to where you can barely see the tips of the drum sticks. Now imagine being able to *think* that fast, following and feeling every stroke and impact with exacting clarity and comprehension.

With this single exercise, my hands were soon able to move at a pace almost equal to my thinking, leaving few ideas unreleased or behind. It also accelerated my ability to comprehend fast, complex rhythm passages, far beyond what I'd been capable of grasping up to that point.

Remember that at the time, all I cared about was getting this unnamed "thing" out of my system. When I could play so fast that I was ready to pass out, the temporary exorcism was achieved, only to have the proverbial demons return all too soon. Finesse would come later, with many years of practice.

But it wasn't just the physical speed that excited me; it was the *mental* speed as well, along with the associated thought processes, that released waves of endorphins (mood-improving chemicals).

And this is a *very* important point...

Being able to express and execute musical thoughts at such a high rate electrifies your body with energy and adrenaline. The quicker your mind can move, the more amazing the patterns you can create and experience. Ken Rosenberg's six-stroke roll exercise didn't just accelerate my hands; it threw fuel on the fire of my already racing mind.

Thank you, Ken!

Tourette Syndrome and Music

A lot is said about the lack of musicality inherent in playing something fast, but for people with Tourette's, we are actually speaking the language of rhythm at a pace that is relatively normal. Developing and nurturing this instant connectivity is what primarily lead to the drum set becoming a powerful tool for my tension and endorphin release.

The stronger my hands and feet became, the more endurance they gained. I really was approaching the drum set now as an athletic pursuit, which was about as close to becoming good in any sport as I would ever get. I used dumbbells, wrist grips, and oversized metal drum sticks to build the strength and endurance in my hands, and I also wore ankle weights on my feet to build up my skinny legs. I really was determined to turn myself into a living, breathing drumming machine, and slowly but surely, that's exactly what I was becoming...

/ /

By my mid-teen years, the drum set was now fully serving as both physical and musical therapy, all in the name of trying to escape the nameless intruder. The downside of such a focus on the physical was the increased isolation due to hours of practice. I literally wanted to be the best drummer in the world, but I pursued this lofty goal at the expense of not achieving a balance with other life interests.

My self-esteem hinged upon unleashing a display on the drum set that would bring applause, and while I was able to socialize with other musicians and develop friendships, the desire to leap far beyond them actually made drumming too much of a good thing. It should have definitely been more about becoming a better musician.

But I didn't and probably couldn't have recognized this, because time spent away from the drums brought me ever-presently back to the never-ending reality of not knowing why my body was exhibiting its constant spastic behavior. Most every day was spent at some point wondering, "Why is my body *doing* this? Will I *ever* find the answer?"

Any pursuit that took me away from being obsessed with answering those two questions was usually done in excess. The benefits of having so much musical talent were healing for the soul, but sometimes it was a showboating bandage at best. Not knowing the answers was an endless test of sanity and faith. Still, without music and drumming, I've little doubt my path would have strayed, and I'd have flailed aimlessly.

/ /

During this time (ninth grade), I really grew as a musician, not just as a drummer, but also through exploration of the electric guitar, acoustic piano, and bass guitar. However, my attention and focus were still weak, making the reading of tonal music a very difficult task.

My drum set reading had improved through my lessons with Mr. Kenny, but I had great difficulty making sense of music staffs with flats, sharps, bass and treble clefs, and everything else that came along with the tonal world. I played the instruments mostly by ear, something for which I seemed to have a knack, but I *do* wish I had slowed everything down and found the patience and focus to have taken piano or guitar lessons from a teacher who could have helped me work to overcome my challenges.

My maternal grandmother bought me a small electric guitar with a practice amp, and I tried to relearn some of the chords I'd studied ten years before. This helped me play a few of my favorite songs, or at least some versions of them. I tried to pick out lead guitar notes, too, but a lot more practice would have been required for things to feel like second nature.

Also around this time, my mother bought my brother Charlie a piano and enrolled him in lessons. He did not have Tourette's and did rather well with reading music. I'd sit down sometimes and give it a try, but I couldn't make any sense of notes aligned vertically on a page that I had to play horizontally on a keyboard.

Regardless, as with the guitar, I was able to have a lot of fun just playing by ear and exploring chord combinations. I would say too that the percussive nature of the piano fit in very well with the rhythm skills I was developing on the drums. And while I wasn't very good at *reading* music, I did learn how to *write* it, VERY SLOWLY. Soon I was able to create simple compositions on the piano and put them onto paper, aided by taking a high school music theory class.

I also decided to give the bass guitar a shot, to better understand how to interact with the bass player in bands. The throbbing low frequency vibrations felt very pleasant, and both the piano and the bass guitar improved my disposition, adding another musical dimension to experience relief from. The percussive nature of the electric bass and acoustic piano often required powerful finger action, but strumming the thick bass guitar strings or gently gracing the ivory keys produced equally relaxing sensations. More on this in Part II.

/ /

As I looked forward wondering what my music future would hold, I never stopped believing I'd find the answer I needed regarding my uninvited neurological visitor. But I was trying to figure out a machine with no blueprint, no manual, and no clue. It was... maddening.

Everything I learned was done through trial and error, but that's not to say it was all bad. I discovered aspects of neurology and music that amaze me to this day, and in our next chapter, we'll dive into the mystery and magic of fusing mind and body.

Chapter 8

Momentum

With involuntary motor movements and vocalizations plaguing me during my teen years, I was obsessed with finding the origins from within. As self-awareness and consciousness evolved, I became fascinated with seeking the source of the streaming rhythm patterns. Their complexity and precision went far beyond a "simple boom-tap, boom-tap."

I was thinking in multi-layered musical terms and unleashing torrents of explosive drum fills across the set, somehow always landing on the beat. I wanted to know *how* I was able to do this, and I also wanted to know *where* the patterns and impulses were coming from. My thought was that if I could somehow find the musical source, I might be able to get closer to helping doctors understand the organic (physical) source of my unexplained nervous movements.

In time, I would eventually realize that the physical obsessive-compulsive component of Tourette's was actually serving as a great asset in terms of the conception and execution of these elaborately complex rhythm patterns and fills. Truly, this was the last thing I would have ever imagined, and the disability was showing itself to be even more of an ability, in some very unexpected ways.

Remember *palilalia*, the involuntary repetition of one's own words, and *echolalia*, the repeating of other peoples' words and sounds? The palilalia aspect let me take and repeat an internal musical theme, and echolalia let me take and mimic an external musical theme. These repetition tools became a great creative and structural asset around which I could then add drum fill variations extending well beyond a single measure of time.

I experienced tremendous physical pleasure when executing these increasingly elaborate rhythm patterns. They released waves of endorphins that became quite addicting, much to the frustration of fellow musicians who surely wished I'd simply just kept the beat. However, *they* weren't hearing or feeling what I was experiencing. Those ideas absolutely demanded release, and to me, they were valid music events.

The impulses to play these complex patterns were mostly not of my conscious doing or making. Regardless, when I *did* give them the "green light" and let them loose, my neural pathways were wired for such instantaneous execution of movement signals that the slightest thought (conscious or otherwise) quickly became percussive reality.

The stream of consciousness I connected with was ecstasy when it flowed, and I could create sheets of sound, a phrase borrowed from a *DownBeat* article I once read describing John Coltrane's sax playing. I loved that description, because the waves of rhythm patterns really *did* flow with no effort. All I had to do was let them out and let them become music.

Those impulses were often a ride extending well beyond a single measure. They seemed to leap out of my hands and feet, and as mentioned earlier, somehow, I physically knew *exactly* where they would end up within the music, even though I hadn't consciously created them. The patterns inspired variations on themselves, which I intuitively knew how to interject at points not always on the beat and well beyond. I just let my mind and muscles move randomly, discovering new sounds along the way, loving every minute of it.

/ /

The real challenge was to manage this flow and direct it. As I wrote about in "Rhythm Man," I'd spend the rest of my life striving to master that aspect of performance. I remain fascinated by the process, because it takes me away from the unwanted movements of Tourette's, and if there was ever an argument supporting the use of music as a from of treatment for Tourette's, experiencing the "flow" is it.

This aided greatly in exploring jazz improvisation, where one was encouraged to let go and discover. The physical aspects of Tourette's remained the same, but I also had new drumming influences to help offset the ever-present stress and anxiety of not knowing what was going on with my body.

Peter Erskine played with Stan Kenton, and later with Weather Report. He was a rising young jazz star with a rock sensibility, and his drumming was always intentional, deliberate, and tasteful. He put one-hundred percent of himself into every beat and cymbal tap, with a level of concentration I could only hope to gain a small piece of. I first met Peter at the Stan Kenton summer jazz clinics at Towson State University when I was in high school, and then a few years later in Los Angeles, where I was able to study privately with him.

Taking lessons from one of your drumming idols is like going to sports camp with your favorite baseball players. It never seems real, but it sure is informative! Peter's focus on playing the drums musically really imprinted on me, and his patience with the instrument is something that any drummer (or any musician, for that matter) can learn a great deal from.

Lenny White was another strong drumming influence, and I remember hearing him for the first time on my sixteenth birthday, when he was playing with Chick Corea and Return to Forever. Lenny used a large, white Gretsch kit, and he played unlike anyone I'd ever seen or heard. It was a life-transforming experience to witness his extraordinary ability to explore the drums as a true musical instrument.

Lenny was a "lefty," so his kit was set up the opposite of most drummers. He too had no real formal training on the drums, and as an art student, he seemed to explore the palette of sounds on the drum set the way a painter would dabble with colors. His flam triplets remain one of my favorite fills.

Lenny made a comment once in *DownBeat* about how some drummers play from the top down, meaning they focus on their hands first, then their feet. He also mentioned that other drummers play from the bottom up, meaning they focus on their feet first, and then their hands. That comment really sank in and helped change my playing, especially in later years when I actually focused on keeping a solid beat by playing feet-first, from the "bottom up."

Tony Williams was only seventeen when he joined trumpeter Miles Davis, which floored me, because I was seventeen when I discovered both of these jazz giants. Tony was a non-stop motion machine who played with more musical intensity and composition than anyone I'd ever heard. His melodies flowed out over the drums, and he'd lead the charge a few years earlier to develop one of the most influential jazz/rock trios ever, with The Tony Williams Lifetime.

There were drummers who were faster, but none who were more musical and compositional. Tony slammed hard, yet he could just as quickly drop to whisper-quiet and feather-light. Tony played a darker sounding set of K. Zildjian cymbals, and their shades were something he really knew how to make art with. Drummers are *still* listening to his cymbal work to understand it. Tony Williams was also an inspiration because he was a drummer, composer, and band leader, much like the next drummer, who shaped my rhythmic world the most.

Billy Cobham earned his place in the drumming history books by playing with legendary odd time signature explorer/electric guitarist John McLaughlin. Cobham later established himself as a composer and band leader, a notion that further inspired my own hopes of those pursuits. By way of his intense odd meter explorations and boldness to embrace the drum set as a musical instrument *far* beyond that of a mere metronome,

Tourette Syndrome and Music

Billy Cobham opened doors of musical discovery that permanently fused the drum set with my case of Tourette's.

His jazz drumming incorporated syncopation, where accents are placed on weaker beats within the music. His unexpected placement of these accents was roughly the musical equivalent of Tourette's unexpected nature, with pops and kicks occurring to knock the listener off balance.

My body was doing the *very* same thing to me virtually every waking moment, and it was through jazz drumming improvisation, inspired by Cobham's mastery and injection of the unexpected, that I found my most potent and informally beneficial music therapy realizations.

I wanted to mimic Cobham's drumming and his Gatling-gun intensity, because the same kind of energy that drove his drumming was occurring beneath my skin and within my head. Now those events had an energy voice to be expressed with, and I found that by attempting to develop the technique required to imitate this master drummer, I forged connections between my mind and body that helped refine and further the release and expression of the stress brought on by Tourette's.

Doing so also raised the bar on my own drumming expectations. Many years later, I wrote Cobham and actually got a reply after thanking him for being such an inspiration during my uncertain and confusing high school years. He simply replied, "Glad to be of some positive resource in your life. Bill C."

I will never erase that e-mail.

Tourette Syndrome and Music

Another aspect of jazz, specifically John McLaughlin's odd time signature compositions, also seemed to mirror my inner world. These compositions were not constructed of the usual four beats to the measure I'd been playing for years. Instead, they consisted of 5, 7, 9, 11 and more, creating unusual temporal contours that my body definitely related to, due to their unconventional nature and the unexpected occurrence of the downbeat.

This music was formally introduced to me in a jazz band performance context by Hank Levy, a Baltimore jazz composer and university professor who was visiting our high school on a government arts grant. Hank Levy, in no uncertain terms, was the educator who would most deeply shape my musical direction and exploration. Hank had played baritone sax in the Stan Kenton Orchestra and had written for Kenton and Don Ellis, both of whom were also odd meter explorers.

Hank's enthusiasm and energy was gruff and to the point. He loved bringing the "roar" out of musicians, and he served as a perfect conduit for all I was experiencing. Hank accepted my then undiagnosed Tourette's, which in turn helped *me* accept it, because all he cared about was making the music the best it could be, and he excelled in bringing that out of all of us.

Hank specialized in odd meter compositions, and his time explorations forced our young minds to embrace exciting new music challenges. He taught us that by combining the basic timekeeping elements of two and three beats per measure, a seamless construction of any odd meter beat could be achieved. I spent hours practicing such combinations, and while doing so, discovered another most unusual therapeutic aspect of music.

/ /

One afternoon during my junior year in high school, I was drumming in my basement, playing an improvised rock beat with eleven beats to the measure. It was divided 8 + 3, and while repeating a simple pattern, a memory formed in my mind of a drive through the mountains of Puerto Rico while visiting my maternal grandfather (the one who sent my brother Charlie and I the native percussion instruments when we lived in Texas).

Imagery began to unfold freely, accompanied by nothing more than a drum beat. It was a vivid experience, and I closed my eyes and just dissolved into it. What I discovered that day was the trance state, induced by the repetition of a beat. By entering that state, I released myself *from* myself and let subconsciously-driven rhythms completely take over, stimulating whatever they might in the process.

Up to that point, I had been turning over my body to music. Now, I turned over my *mind* and body, completely surrendering to what was happening with the beat. I granted permission for my soul and all the mental processes to move and be moved. In doing so, I let my mind tell stories while

Tourette Syndrome and Music

staying out of its way as it spoke. Playing with eyes closed and turning my head from side to side seemed to stimulate the inner ears' balancing system, with powerful image-inducing results. I felt my head spin and my body fall and rise, and as I let my hands fly off the drums and cymbals with no restraint, movement ignited more movement.

Neurons fired, life erupted in my head, and I experienced vivid images, colors, sounds, physical sensations and memories. It was miles beyond surreal. It was utterly awesome.

It was the real musical deal.

From that day forward, no matter what Tourette Syndrome sought to serve up, I had at last found a way to escape it, and at the same time, let it be, which in turn, let *me* be me.

And that, I could live with.

Tourette Syndrome and Music

Chapter 9

Where The Road Began To Lead

Discovering the deeper neuro-physical aspects of drumming and improvisation added a great deal of color to my nervous world. On a more grounded level, involvement with other musicians helped me develop confidence to let my ever-present guard down. I'm absolutely sure that 100% of the Tourette readership knows *exactly* what I'm talking about...

Before you were diagnosed, you likely often wondered if people were always looking at you, as you asked yourself, "What is the *matter* with me?" Add to that the frustration of not being able to tell them what *was* wrong, because you didn't know, and a picture forms of what my school years were like.

With music, a shield of sorts developed that eased the staring and inquiry. For parents considering involving their kids in music, let me say and repeat that the benefits and emotional release are invaluable. The interaction with others and the participation without fear are elements of growing up that all kids should know as much of as they can. Both build inner strength and confidence, and music provided me with many such experiences.

The symphonic, marching, and jazz bands in high school opened many more doors for personal growth and confidence building. All three bands traveled to play in competitions around Delaware, and occasionally we even went out of state. Two particular experiences from marching band really stand out, one of which involved writing a drum cadence that the percussion section played to energize the home audience.

I wrote it in ninth grade, and long after I left Glasgow High School, it was still being played. It was a duet of sorts between the snare drums and the bass drums, with fills provided by the smaller tom-toms and cymbals. We'd all be flailing away, the audience would be clapping their hands and stamping their feet in the grandstands, and I have to tell you, it really was quite entertaining to hear it all going on and thinking that the noise first began as a simple idea I heard in my head.

A second memory from that time crowned the whole marching band experience on one very high-energy afternoon. Glasgow's football team won the state championship with a down-to-the-last-minute play or two, and the marching band in the stands was wailing away to support them.

As the game's outcome became closer and closer, the percussion section slammed louder and louder. There were no limits; we were all hitting our drums and cymbals as hard as we could, driving everyone around us into an even greater level of frenzy. When we finally won, the lid blew off the powder keg, and we were all screaming at the top our lungs in support of our humble little team.

I felt this kind of energy all the time, and I tried to keep it contained. Now I could let it loose without apology! I'd never known such a powerful release that was both socially acceptable and encouraged; I would only experience this level of music-related release one more time in high school, an event I wrote about in "Rhythm Man," after a life-changing drum solo performance.

The fun of being in marching band also came from playing several different types of drums over the four years in high school. Strapping on the marching bass drum in ninth grade felt inferior at first, because my hands and ambitions were aimed at the marching snare drum. I made the most of it though, smacking the big heads on that fat, shiny chrome drum with my wooden mallets as hard as I could. It became physical music therapy at its finest!

During my junior year, we mounted three very large and heavy stainless-steel Ludwig timp-toms onto a rolling cart that strapped to my shoulders. The timp-toms were too heavy for anyone to carry any length of time, so the cart was a welcome aid, and I assaulted them unmercifully! Wailing away on those three drums was pure ecstasy, providing me with tremendous release and relief.

I should include mention here of attending the West Chester State University summer marching band camp sessions my freshman and sophomore years in high school. I developed a deeper appreciation of rudimental drumming thanks to the wonderful sessions provided by Willis M. Rapp. He introduced us to a much wider variety of international rudiments (classic snare drumming patterns) that expanded my performing vocabulary quite a bit, especially the swiss triplets.

Tourette Syndrome and Music

I loved the way Mr. Rapp wrote cadences (groups of drumming patterns), because it gave me my first taste of learning composition. I really grew from those summer studies; they took me deeper into the form of drumming that would provide me with the speed and power I needed for complete expression.

But rudimental drumming also taught me the discipline of practice and focus. Without these two elements that were critical to this form of music, I'm not sure I would have learned either as well elsewhere.

Senior year led to me finally joining the snare drum line, and we developed cadences and routines that gave the rest of the state high school bands a good percussive run for their money. I taught the other drummers some of my fast hand tricks, and we never failed to put on quite a show. Excelling in something like this really helped build my confidence in the face of constant self-doubt. Respect from peers, friends, and teachers all contributed to raising my usually beaten-down self-esteem into a head's up position.

The involvement with symphonic band demanded a great deal of concentration to follow the written music, but I can't say my concentration was always up for the task. I was therefore shocked to walk into school one Monday and see my name up on the band homeroom chalkboard as having been chosen first chair (lead drummer) for the Delaware All-State Symphonic Band. This also automatically placed me as first chair for the Delaware All-State Orchestra.

Tourette Syndrome and Music

It's worth sharing this story because it has to do with quitting and then getting back up on the horse. I'd been practicing a piece called "2040 Sortie," a very challenging snare drum solo that let my hands do what they did best: play very fast. But towards the time of the actual audition, I lost my self-confidence and was terrified at the idea of auditioning in front of three judges. I did NOT want people staring at me in a small band room, checking out my every movement.

My percussion tutor, Richard Tull, was Glasgow's assistant band director, and he really did do his best to get me into drumming shape. But honestly, my expectation and fear were stronger than his belief, and I finally put down my sticks, giving up without even going in to see how I would do.

I was also having a very rough senior year with a lot of personal problems, and they added to the overwhelming feelings of doubt. These moments come with any teenage territory, but having Tourette's only made it worse. I can't remember exactly what made me finally go to the audition, but it was the first major moment in my life where I recall challenging fear and going ahead anyway.

The audition actually turned out to be not so bad, and I remember thinking when I was done how silly it was to have gotten so worked up over it all. Needless to say, I was still shocked to walk into school after that weekend and see my name on the board, at the top. The lesson learned really was simple: go for it and see what happens, because the outcome might *really* surprise you.

Three additional music highlights also occurred in my senior year. The first was earning first chair in the Delaware All-State Jazz Band, led by my musical mentor, composer Hank Levy. The second was a "Most Improved Musician" award, based on hardly being able to read music in ninth grade to earning some serious respect along the way. No one really knew how difficult it was for me to live with Tourette's, nor how challenging it was to try and focus on becoming better at anything. And at the time, I could not tell them why.

The third highlight was a dream come true: traveling to Europe on the road with a band. Director Hal Schiff founded and organized the American Youth Jazz Band to showcase young players and to exchange international goodwill. Hal Schiff was an incredibly patient, supportive, and understanding musician and educator, who took kids under his wing and nurtured them.

Playing in the American Youth Jazz Band (AYJB) was an extraordinary experience, and I was one of two drummers in the group, along with Eric Blomstrom. Eric was a really good guy, and we shared drumming duties in a way that taught me a lot about musical teamwork. The AYJB performed in the Delaware and Pennsylvania area on TV and radio, with live performances at outdoor arenas as well, in addition to recording a live album.

In Europe, we performed in Switzerland, Germany, Luxembourg, and Scotland, with appearances on German television. Some of the real thrills included playing on the beautiful shores of Lake Montreux in Switzerland, and performing outdoors at the base of the massively gothic cathedral in Koln, Germany.

To be a part of that group at eighteen was a ride that's hard to describe. I still hadn't received a correct diagnosis, but I had a girlfriend in the band, was seeing the world, and was learning how to best adapt to life with an unknown nervous disorder. If playing jazz taught me anything, it was how to improvise and make the most of whatever got thrown my way.

It really is true what they say about show business: no matter what happens, the show must go on. That's what I learned and loved about high school music involvement. And in every sense, a disability continued to reveal itself to be an ability, offering more opportunities than limitations.

Chapter 10

Playin' Inna Rock 'n' Roll Band

This journey down musical memory lane wouldn't be complete without mentioning a few of the bands I played in during my middle and high school years and sharing some other music experiences that shaped my world. So, we're going to step back a little in the time line, and then continue forward.

By eighth grade, my playing had developed enough that I felt confident to answer ads for musicians in the local paper. I connected with a rhythm guitar player named Travis, who was working with a lead guitarist named Nathan. They lived about ten miles north of me, and my mom was a truly good sport to haul me and my drums to the rehearsals.

We set up in Nathan's garage and went through some rock and blues tunes, and as so many legendary groups before us had no doubt done, we eventually held a post-rehearsal circle to ask the sacred and time-honored question:

"So... ya wanna form a band?"

And form one we did, minus a bass player. *Those* guys were almost impossible to find, but we pressed on regardless, calling ourselves "Axis." I colored my bass drum head with magic marker artwork and created a logo in the classic tradition of all awesome rock bands, because that we were!

I'm pretty sure we only ever played one party. Mostly, we just rehearsed and tried to make music. I loved playing loud and fast, and so did Nathan. He had a beautiful cherry-red Gretsch hollow body guitar, and that guy could play "Johnny Be Good" like he wrote it! The band didn't last long due to the driving distance, but for a couple of months, I was, in my own Tourette-inflamed mind, a gen-u-ine rock star.

/ /

The summer of eighth grade, I met Diane Vaccaro and her brothers, Bruce and Jay. Diane was a singer and keyboard player, and Bruce played rhythm guitar. Jay was an electronics whiz, so he became our sound man. Diane and Bruce were older than me, out of high school, working real jobs, and I felt kind of privileged to hang out and play with adults. Plus, they didn't mind my Tourette's at all. They just figured I was a very hyperactive guy who *needed* to be behind a drum set. That acceptance from older musicians desperately helped shore up my general lack of confidence.

We played the music of the day, the 70's glam rock and heavy metal, and we gave it a decent shot. Diane eventually moved on with her music, and shortly after that, I discovered the blazing fingers of lead guitarist Al Raddick one day as I was walking home. I heard the most incredible electric guitar sounds coming out of an upstairs window, so I walked up to the door and knocked.

Al and I hit it off from the first hellos, and he joined our unnamed band shortly thereafter. He had amazing guitar skills, and he loved that I wanted to play like a bat with its wings on fire. We dove headfirst into Led Zeppelin, Black Sabbath, David Bowie, Deep Purple... all the groups I'd been listening to! One group from Holland called Focus had a one-hit wonder with their single, "Hocus Pocus." I loved that song, because it let the drums cut loose and solo right in the middle. Whenever the band asked me what I wanted to play, *that* was the tune I called.

My brother and mother were incredibly accommodating when the guys would come over to rehearse. I unleashed enough energy in those evenings to drive the electrical needs of a small town. My marching band drumming abilities had given my hands the speed and strength to blaze for hours, and my feet were equally powerful and fast.

I was a rock and roll drummer in every sense with these guys, and while I kind of put musicality aside, I let energy and showmanship come front and center. Our little unnamed band added other players along the way, played a few parties, had fun, and just lived for making music. There was a raw purity to it that I will always love and remember, because it was what making music was all about: *just playing*.

But on at least one occasion, I made more spectacle than music. We were playing at an outdoor party, and I was given a drum solo. I went completely insane, pulling out every trick I knew, diving into a pool of drumming self-indulgence. Afterwards, when the band was taking a break, I was talking with the girlfriend of one of the guitar players. I was expecting her to tell me how great I sounded, but instead, she bluntly told me that she thought I was a musical jerk. It was a very good and needed reality check, because being able to play certain things doesn't mean you always *should*. Real music is often made by leaving more space for the other players to say something, and clearly, sometimes it's better to say a lot less.

/ /

There were three high school musicians who formed the core of deep musical friendships that tapped into rock as well as jazz roots. Paul Harlyn played keyboards, and along with Mark Wallace on bass and Chris McDermott on guitar, we would get together to explore more advanced progressive rock. I had a lot of cool musical moments with these artists, who still play professionally.

And certainly, I have to mention the very first rock concert I ever went to. Stan Levin, my "big brother," whom I met through Big Brothers of America, took me to see Dave Mason and Joe Cocker at the Spectrum in Philadelphia for my 13th birthday. I will never forget the intensity and the volume of that performance, and if anything convinced me I should be up on a stage playing the drums, that concert was it.

Stan played a 6 and 12-string guitar, really loved music, and he was all for diving in to see where I could go with drumming. I have been forever grateful for the encouragement and guidance he provided me.

Tourette Syndrome and Music

Those of you who've read "Rhythm Man" know what a special night it was that the story led up to, and while it was not a rock band evening, the energy certainly was, drawing deeply from my high amplitude inclinations. The drum solo I wrote about threw me headfirst into the performance spotlight and forced me to adapt with every bit of musical skill and volume I had to keep from getting lost in the pace. I had never experienced anything like the surge of energy from that song ("Quiet Friday") or any other song, for that matter.

The performance was the defining moment of my musical life. It left me bare, exposed to the world, and filled with adrenaline. Handling those raw, blazing moments really showed me what a profound level of control I could achieve, and I have drawn from that experience often over the years. I definitely fused jazz and rock that night, oh yes...

/ /

I wouldn't say I outgrew playing rock, and I still love it, but jazz seemed to let me go further in terms of certain explorations regarding advanced rhythmic concepts. The more I fed my soul with this genre of music, the more I seemed to grow. A big part of this evolution occurred during high school graduation week, when both my dad and my maternal grandfather came to town.

My grandfather was born and raised in Puerto Rico, and I loved him more than words can say. Things were always rough with my dad, who also had an undiagnosed case of mild Tourette's we'd later discover. But I never felt as close to him as I did my grandfather, who grew floral cuttings in the mountains of Puerto Rico.

He had a poet's wisdom, and when he spoke, he had thought out very deeply whatever he'd wanted to say. It was always his hope to have a musician in the family, and he was quite thrilled one morning during his visit to be able to watch me on TV, playing with a local jazz group. He sat quietly through the show, and when it was done, he told me two things.

"The trumpet player is a nervous boy."

"How do you know that?" I asked.

"He chews his fingernails," my grandfather replied.

His next words gave me the final stamp of approval I needed to expand and embark on my life's musical journey.

"And you have the heart and soul of an artist."

He then handed me a one-hundred dollar bill, and I knew *exactly* what to do with it...

Later that week, after digging through all of my issues of *DownBeat* magazine (a jazz publication that I eventually wrote a piece for about a percussionist named Vinx, in 1992), I noted every five star-rated album I could find and headed downtown to Wonderland Records with some additional graduation gift money from my dad to fill a shopping basket with a wide range of study materials.

As you can see, up to this point, I had been going at drumming with a lot of energy, but not much specific focus.

After weighing my grandfather's words, I came to the realization that without question, even as much as I loved playing rock and roll, the time had come to really study my craft, to fully nurture my jazz side, and to get very serious about becoming a musician.

And get serious I did.

Tourette Syndrome and Music

Chapter 11

College and Something *Quite* Beyond

I graduated from Glasgow High School in 1977, toured Europe that summer with the American Youth Jazz Band, and enrolled as a music major at Towson State College (now Towson State University) in the fall. I was following my dream of studying with Hank Levy, the jazz composer who'd introduced me to his unique brand of odd meter jazz just a few years earlier.

Hank had encouraged all of us in the high school jazz band to attend summer music camps at Towson, hosted by Stan Kenton and his Orchestra. This had given me a cool introduction to the campus, and I really looked forward to exploring odd meters there further.

Hank Levy was, and remains, the most powerful influence in my musical world. He accepted me for who I was and what I had, and he gave me very solid direction. Wondering for fourteen years why you can't sit still and why you make strange noises and movements would take a toll on anyone's focus. With Hank, as anyone who played under him can attest, there was nothing *but* focus.

We used to have great talks about music in his office at Towson, and he always greeted me with a smile. An alumni band exists in Baltimore that plays Hank's music today, and they carry a powerful legacy. But this is not to say that Hank was always easy going. His band rehearsals were demanding and intense, and for someone with concentration issues such as myself, he had the perfect remedy: if you weren't giving Hank your all, he'd throw a felt chalkboard eraser you way, and he *rarely* missed. I never had to dodge one, but the threat of it sure kept us all on our toes!

I still had not received a proper diagnosis of Tourette's, so, the general confusion level remained fairly high. Adjusting to college, being away from home, and living in a dorm were not easy changes to make. Becoming a full-time music major was a huge transition from goofing off in high school, but as always, being around musicians felt comfortable and safe.

However, my ADD made it very difficult for me to focus and read music at the level required for college, and I was barely keeping up. I could play and improvise, but reading never came easy. It was frustrating, because I really wanted to play for a living. I lasted only one semester before switching to psychology, and I half-hoped that making this academic change would help me figure out why my body was doing all the things it was doing without my consent.

But I was by no means done with music.

I would sometimes sit in at local jazz clubs just to get thrown into the middle of things. The leader would call a tune for us to play, and we'd barely have a few seconds to collect our thoughts before the music began. That was always a thrill, having to meet the challenge of the unexpected.

As I have mentioned a few times, this was very much what Tourette's did to me every day: throw one challenge after another after another. And for some reason, I craved these adapting experiences, almost as much as I longed for a proper diagnosis. I can't explain the former, but when the latter finally arrived, my entire world changed.

/ /

In January, 1979, while I was home from school on winter break, I was watching *The Tonight Show*, as I often did to check out drummer Ed Shaughnessy. On that particular night, a public service announcement came on that stopped me dead in my tracks, because it was like hearing someone speak a language that you knew but had never heard another soul utter a word of.

A young man about my age was on the screen, exhibiting many of the symptoms I'd had most of my life.

I copied down the contact information for the National Tourette Syndrome Association in New York City and called them the next day. They referred me to Dr. Harvey Singer, a pediatric neurologist at John Hopkins University, in Baltimore, and I made an appointment that week. I wanted to be seen by a pediatric neurologist because I thought he might more quickly recognize my current symptoms and my description of the ones I'd had during my childhood. And, I did *not* want to make the same mistake I had made just two years earlier.

When I was a senior in high school in Delaware, my mother brought home a brochure from the dentist's office one day that described Tourette's and its symptoms. It seemed like the real deal, and we got very excited, but I was not so sure.

We made an appointment with a neurologist in Wilmington, up the road from my home in Newark, but on the day we went in, he was not available. His associate saw us instead, and unfortunately, he was not as familiar with Tourette's.

At this point in my life, I was extremely self-conscious, and as a result, the control I had developed over my body went into overdrive, letting very few come symptoms out. This really backfired on me, because in the doctor's eyes, I clearly did NOT have Tourette's. He even made a point of mentioning that I didn't swear. Only a small portion of the Tourette population actually have coprolalia, and I was not one of them, so it didn't even matter.

What *did* matter was that I missed an opportunity to receive anything even close to an accurate diagnosis for the first time. The doctor gave us the name of a psychiatrist whom I saw briefly, but she was equally uninformed, stating that I could not possibly have been suffering from Tourette's because my arms and legs did not flail about uncontrollably.

No, they did not... *precisely because of the control derived from playing the drums*. Again, a backfire. I remember my mother asking me on the way home why I didn't let the first doctor see my symptoms. The answer was simple: it was just too embarrassing for me to let it all out.

I can't over-emphasize how much this holding-back moment derailed the diagnosis process that'd been twelve years in the making. If I'd just let it all out, those two delayed years could've hastened the transformation from living with an unknown neurological disorder to moving forward with the most valuable piece of information I could have hope for.

If only...

Needless to say, when I walked into Dr. Singer's office, I made sure that I shared *every* piece of information I could recount about my childhood experiences. I let the tics come out as well, something I was well versed in restraining.

It was not so hard this time to deal with being observed; Dr. Singer and his associate asked a lot of detailed questions, and I really enjoyed opening up to these professionals. I wanted this thing to have a name, and I was looking to them to tell me why I could not sit still, could not stop moving, could not simply *be*.

Dr. Singer took some blood to test to see if I had anything that might be mimicking Tourette's, and when I went back a week later, he confirmed that in his opinion, based on observation and historical recounting of my experiences, I did indeed have Tourette Syndrome.

I slept well that night... and the next day, my new life began.

Chapter 12

Julius Wechter

Armed with my newfound diagnosis after a maddening fourteen-year search, I awoke feeling like sanity had perched itself back on my shoulder, asking me, "So... now what?"

Music was still my plan, and I could focus on it more than ever before. College, however, just wasn't holding my attention, so I started considering where I wanted to move to play jazz. Philadelphia, Atlantic City, New York... many options ran through my head. I finally settled on a simple goal: I would move to New Haven, Connecticut, and play in college jazz bands led by composer Neil Slater. This would allow me to finish school and stay close to New York City, where jazz thrived and beckoned.

During the summers of 1978 and 1979, I began playing small group jazz in the Philadelphia area with Jim Beard, a pianist I'd met through the American Youth Jazz Band. Jim invited me to join his trio and play classic jazz tunes, which led to an amazing musical education. I owe Jim a great deal for that experience, because he really is the guy who introduced me to small group jazz and all of its subtle sophistication.

Jim eventually went on to become one of the luminaries of jazz piano, even playing and recording with one of my jazz/ fusion idols, guitarist John McLaughlin. Among the many things I learned about music from Jim was that if I was serious about playing jazz, I needed to be where it was happening; hence, my decision to be near New York.

Having just received my proper diagnosis, I had another reason to be near the Big Apple: it was the national headquarters of the Tourette Syndrome Association. I'd stayed in touch with them, and I wanted to put out the word about Tourette's so other kids would not have to go for years like I did without receiving a proper diagnosis.

I recall talking to a woman in the New York office about it over the phone, and I mentioned to her that I was a drummer. She asked me if I had ever heard of Julius Wechter, leader of the Baja Marimba Band. Julius had Tourette's and had been diagnosed late in life. He became involved with the Tourette Syndrome Association and was featured in a short (and now classic) documentary film called, "Stop it! I Can't!"

The name sounded familiar, and then I remembered why: my mother owned several of his record albums! I had listened to them as a kid, but I *never* thought I would have occasion to meet the man. That was about to change very soon.

I got Julius' address and wrote him a letter, introducing myself as a fellow drummer with Tourette's. I was pretty naïve to think that such a famous person would ever write me back, but I included my phone number, just in case. I sent the letter off and didn't give it much more thought.

About a week later, I was getting things in order to take the train up from Delaware to Connecticut to look for a room to rent in New Haven. I remember it was a Friday morning in June, 1979, and the phone rang. My mom called out from downstairs, and I had no clue what was coming...

Julius Wechter was on the other end!

The initial shock left me very numb, but I was able to manage a conversation, and we got along like we'd known each other forever. I had never talked with anyone so famous, and my life would never be the same. Somewhere across the country was another musician, another drummer no less, with Tourette Syndrome.

We spoke again about a week later. Julius told me that if I was ever out in California, I should look him up, and he would introduce me to some musicians around Los Angeles. That was *all* I needed to hear, because the minute we hung up, I said to my mom, "I'm moving to California!"

The next month was pumped with adrenaline as I prepared to leap across country, and shortly after I got out to California in August 1979, I was standing face-to-face with the first person I'd ever met who had Tourette's. I was looking into the eyes of someone who had lived the life and was willing to share some stories and experiences. It was surreal.

We spent the afternoon of our first meeting with Julius' wife, Cissy, and a friend at their Laguna Beach condo. I was looking out over the Pacific Ocean in awe of the leap I'd just made, and we talked about music, Tourette's, and living in general.

My case was not so bad, and in fact, Julius even wondered if I actually had Tourette's! I think I was so relaxed from having driven across country that things had calmed down a bit on the inside. But the irony was never lost on me.

/ /

Once I settled in Los Angeles, I visited Julius at his home, a mansion formerly owned by Mickey Rooney. This was even more surreal. I saw actual gold records on the walls from his work with The Baja Marimba Band as well as with Herb Alpert and the Tijuana Brass. I had never been inside a home like this, and it was hard not to feel completely overwhelmed.

It was a far cry from Delaware...

But, the thing that struck me the most about Julius was that despite his wealth and fame (we're talking about an original member of The Wrecking Crew, for you older fans of 60's hits), he was just another guy with Tourette's. He had fairly mild facial ticks, and we talked a lot about how our tics went away when we played music. It was an incredible experience to finally be able to relate to another human being who was describing much of *me* to me.

Julius was in the process of writing a sound track for *Midnight Madness*, a movie that his son David was directing, and eventually, Julius got very busy, but not before introducing me to some musicians who welcomed me to Los Angeles with great conversation and curiosity.

Drummer Nick Ceroli, whom I mentioned earlier, played for Herb Alpert and the Tijuana Brass, and he was also a very accomplished jazz drummer. Nick's open invitation to join him at big band jazz rehearsals was something I never imagined doing in my life, because here was a guy who was *seriously* famous. But like Julius, Nick treated me like anyone else, and he thought it was pretty cool that I'd just up and moved across country on my own.

Coming to Los Angeles to meet Julius Wechter led to my meeting other famous drummers as well. One night, I went out to a small jazz club called Dante's, where I heard the drummer from *The Tonight Show* when Johnny Carson was the host. Ed Shaughnessy had these huge, mutton-chop sideburns, and this was a guy who had done drum solo battles on the show with Buddy Rich.

Ed knew Hank Levy (my music mentor) very well, so, I walked up and introduced myself on a break. For the rest of that evening, Ed came over to my table after every break, bought me sodas, and we talked about jazz and life. I can't tell you how surreal that evening was, because I was sitting across the table from a guy I'd watched on TV for years!

Thirty-four years later, I was able to return the favor by writing about Ed's back surgery recovery (*David Aldridge's Drumming Blog*, davidaldridge.wordpress.com). I retold the story of how kind this drumming legend had been to me as a kid, and many drummers from around the world sent him get well wishes and cards directly to his hospital room.

None of this would have happened had I not met Julius Wechter, and so much of whom I became as a musician I owe to him. We maintained loose contact over the twenty years I knew him, and in 1992, the result of our meeting came to a wonderful highlight out in Redlands, California, at a Tourette Syndrome support group meeting. It's a day I'll never forget, one that solidified my belief in the therapeutic aspects of music for Tourette's, and we'll take a closer look at that day in Chapter 14.

I had offered to bring my drum set out for kids to play and explore. Julius loaned me several of his personal percussion instruments, and I took them and my drum set out to Redlands for an amazing afternoon. But before we get to that, enough cannot be said about Julius and his interest in helping people with Tourette's.

Julius eventually went back to college to get a degree in counseling, and he worked for many years afterwards with the Los Angeles Tourette Syndrome Association chapter as a volunteer and as its vice-president. His willingness to answer a young, naive stranger's letter from Delaware had an impact that change my life forever and obviously led to much of the ink on these pages.

Julius passed away in 1999, and I will be forever grateful for his first phone call, because it put me on the path to learning that despite having Tourette's, it did not have *me*, and that truly, ANYTHING was possible.

Chapter 13

Adam Ward Seligman

Leaping across country alone to pursue musical dreams was one thing; figuring out how to survive was absolutely another. I'd had a few minimum wage jobs on the East Coast, but now, I had to take care of everything on my own. This would prove to be a serious challenge, because I had definitely not developed any serious money-making skills.

The competition for music jobs in Los Angeles was far more intense than I could have imagined, and I had only just learned about Tourette's. This meant I was adjusting to two significant realities: becoming an independent young adult, and taking on the real business end of the music world. I did not have much of a plan for either, and in a few months, I hit a wall of frustration.

Fortunately, I became aware of another person with Tourette's who would show me greater examples of not quitting than anyone I'd ever known or have known since. He inspired me to never give up because of Tourette's or anything else. The guy was simply unstoppable.

I met Adam Ward Seligman shortly after moving to Los Angeles while attending my first Tourette Syndrome Support group meeting. No book written about music and Tourette Syndrome would or could be complete without mentioning one of Tourette's most determined advocates for disability rights, who also shared a love of music and drumming. Adam and I hit it off right away, and it wasn't long afterwards that he bought a white, 5-piece Slingerland drum set, based on what I'd told him about how playing had helped me gain better control over my mind and body.

I gave Adam some basic lessons, and he really took to drumming. His enthusiasm was infectious, and he was so excited every time he played. We used to set up dual kits and just improvise to see where the musical moments would lead, and we loved it. Adam's original kit is now owned and played by his niece, Sofia Campos-Seligman, who says that thanks to Adam, drumming continues to run in her family.

/ /

Adam was also a writer. His career began with a 1988 piece called "Beating Drums, Beating Disabilities," for *Modern Drummer* (issue #100). His books include *Echolalia* (Hope Press), a novel about a writer with Tourette's, and the now classic, *Don't Think About Monkeys: Extraordinary Stories Written by People with Tourette Syndrome* (Hope Press), co-written by John S. Hilkevich

Adam co-wrote *THE MARRIAGE VOW: Poetry & Reflections Celebrating the Married Life*, a collection of poetry, with his wife Julie Ann Wilde, and *REQUIEM FOR ORPHEUS: An Elegy in Honor of Jaco Pastorius' Forty-Fifth Birthday,* both printed by his company, Echolalia Press.

Tourette Syndrome and Music

I learned a great deal about pushing past whatever life dealt me by watching Adam's examples. He had a very intense case of Tourette's, but he never let it stop him. Adam's life was big, with many projects always going on at once. Adam was the technical consultant to several Tourette Syndrome-related TV episodes that helped put the disorder on the media map, including shows like *L.A. Law*.

He was also instrumental in helping get federal legislation passed regarding the manufacture of drugs for small population groups, like people with Tourette's. At the time, many drug companies would not manufacture certain drugs, because the population and profit margins just didn't hold up in their overall business plans. Adam testified before Congress about it, and an episode of *Quincy* was written specifically to address this issue.

Adam had a way of getting things done, that's for sure, and playing the drums was welcome relief for him from the intensity of his life. I enjoyed jamming with Adam, exploring drums and rhythms in a way that was quite unique. I would sometimes just keep a beat while he flailed and pounded, watching him savor the freedom that comes with expression and exploration. The smile on his face and the peace he found was priceless. Looking back, I can honestly say that I saw in Adam a true and pure love of drumming.

In 1992, Adam and I became screenwriting partners, and we spent time creating pitch ideas and taking meetings with the producers of *Star Trek: The Next Generation*. We never sold anything, but they always invited us back. Quite an honor, considering that at the time, it was the hardest show to write for on television.

What I would like to emphasize for those of you with Tourette's is that pushing forward past your perceived limitations can yield results beyond your wildest dreams. My confidence came from playing music; Adam's came from his success as a writer (he was also a member of the Writers Guild of America). Whatever gives you that boost, take it and run with it.

Music became a huge part of Adam's life when he began working as a recording artist publicist and music journalist. *Weather Report* co-founder Joe Zawinul called Adam "a real gentleman." An accolade like that coming from one of the foremost jazz pianists in the world speaks volumes about Adam's character.

Music has given me relief and pleasure for many years. It gave Adam that too, plus a related career. You just never know where the artist path can take you, and if you wanted to find an example of someone who truly benefited from the therapeutic aspects of music, you'd be hard pressed to find a better example than Adam Ward Seligman, who passed away in 1999.

You are missed, my friend.

Chapter 14

The First Tourette Drum Circle?

Had I not moved to California in 1979 and become involved with the Los Angeles chapter of the Tourette Syndrome Association, I might not have had the opportunity to test my belief in just how valuable drumming had been in helping me deal with Tourette's. The following account is a reprint of *"Drumming As Therapy,"* a 1992 newsletter article I wrote for the Southern California Chapter of the Tourette Syndrome Association. It described an afternoon spent with a group of teenagers with Tourette's and how they reacted to being given a chance to freely explore the drum set and hand percussion.

The event was a clinically unstructured and informally unregulated experiment, and my hope was that more academically-regulated sessions and research projects might eventually become realities. They did. Today, over twenty years later, the music research world embraces drumming as a very valid subject for exploration and experimentation.

I had just written "Rhythm Man" for *Don't Think About Monkeys*, and Oliver Sacks (the noted neurologist) specifically mentioned "Rhythm Man" in the foreword as a piece that showed people how they could turn a disability into an ability. Dr. Sacks most recently mentioned this notion again in his book, *Musicophilia: Tales of Music and the Brain*, and my little demonstration many years before had served as a test of sorts for that idea, one that every player in attendance passed with flying rhythmic colors.

At the time of the event and the writing, the idea of drumming circles was just beginning to grow. It has since evolved into a world-wide community, with strong endorsement and support from percussion companies and the counseling professions. Dr. Barry Bittman (Yamaha Music and Wellness Institute, www.yamahainstitute.org) has conducted research into the therapeutic aspects of drumming, demonstrating that an actual positive chemical change occurs in the body.

This notion has also been explored by Remo, Inc. (www.remo.com), with a program called HealthRHYTHMS. Remo is a leading drum head and percussion instrument manufacturer that has led the way in championing the health aspects of recreational drumming, and they introduced me to a class called *Beat the Odds* that helped give me some basic group drumming training that I put to use in very short order.

In the summer and early fall of 2010, and again in the summer of 2012, I led three hand drumming/drum set demonstrations for groups of kids in Southern California with Tourette's, including one smaller event at Remo's Recreational Music Center in North Hollywood, California (www.remormc.org). With great thanks to the generosity of Remo, I was able to use their percussion equipment to create some very positive and helpful experiences for kids and their parents.

In September 2013, I conducted my first international hand drumming/drum set demo, in Birmingham, England, gratefully arranged through John Fitzgerald (Manager, Recreational Music Activities, Remo, Inc.) and Julie Collier from Tourettes Action UK (www.tourettes-action.org.uk). Remo provided Versa drums and Sounds Shapes, and Julie rented a hall and a drum set for me, and I remain eternally grateful for this opportunity.

The performance was aided immeasurably by local drum circle leader Annie Scotney, and Daniel Cameron, a hand drummer and neuroscience researcher from the University of Western Ontario, Canada. The children and parents on hand were every bit as enthused as their American counterparts, further convincing me of the universal benefits of drumming as therapy for Tourette's.

If you'd like to read the blog about it, please go to davidaldridge.wordpress.com and search for "Tourette's Action UK Drum Circle/Drum Set Demo - Sept. 14, 2013".

[Note: As my schedule allows, I'll continue to offer these demonstrations in the Southern California area and beyond. I will also be coordinating travel and performances to include local drum circle leaders when possible. For more information please visit my music website, www.davidaldridge.net]

Like I said, the drum circle community and the idea of drumming as a healing force has grown incredibly, but it was the following account of an opportunity from twenty-two years ago that opened my eyes as to just how transforming the power of playing the drums could really be. It remains one of the most powerful music bonding moments I've ever had.

Tourette Syndrome and Music

Drumming As Therapy

(Originally published in Tourette Syndrome Newsletter, So. CA. Chapter, December 1992, Vol. 1 No. 2)

On October 11, 1992, I believe a little Tourette Syndrome history was made, or better yet, heard. A handful of very enthusiastic kids with Tourette Syndrome joined me in a room at the Loma Linda Medical Center (Redlands, California), and we spent over two hours banging away on my drum set and some borrowed percussion instruments. There were no rules, no time or volume limits, just complete permission to let bodies explore the world of percussion.

I've wanted to test this idea of drums as therapy for Tourette's for over ten years. Thanks to Colleen Wang and Julius Wechter, the idea became a vivid reality. Colleen, head of the Inland Empire Support Group, invited me to speak at her October TSA support group, and she made the necessary arrangements with the Medical Facility. Julius, vice president of the So. Calif. Chapter, bravely loaned me a box of percussion instruments from his personal collection, and I assured him I would replace anything that was broken.

I spoke briefly to the parents, recounting some of my experiences in dealing with and adapting to Tourette's at home, work, and in my personal life. I kept it short because I knew the kids wanted to play the drums. Colleen barely finished saying, "Okay, David, you can take the kids to – " and most of them were running down the hall. They already knew where the action was!

A couple of parents tagged along out of curiosity, and I could hear the drums being played before I ever got into the room. I thought that was a good sign; at least they weren't going to be shy about it. I admired their enthusiasm and courage, because being in a closed room clearly exposes your vulnerabilities. Most of them lost their inhibitions within about thirty seconds of playing the drums.

I spent a few minutes talking about how I play with a group and how I play when I'm by myself. I wanted them to understand that a drummer has a job to do, and it is not the same as just playing for fun and relaxation. I demonstrated some simple rock n' roll beats, played a Latin samba, and then I switched over to what I like to do to relax. So much of learning involves learning to let go, and I wanted them to see how much fun it could be to just play, make mistakes and not care. Sometimes that's when you discover the most amazing stuff, by accident.

After I finished playing, I wondered if my display would have intimidated them a little. Nothing could have been further from their minds, because when I asked who wanted to play first, ALL the hands shot up! I wanted to be fair about letting everyone play, so I told them that each person could play as long as they wanted, and that everyone would get a turn. We had the room to ourselves for two hours, and no one was going to stop us or interrupt us. Suddenly, those kids were in heaven!

None of them owned a drum set, and for most of them it was the first time behind a "kit." The first up was a young boy whose legs couldn't reach the foot pedals from my drum chair. I put him in a smaller chair, and he began to play. His hands went from drums to cymbals, feeling the impact of sticks and reacting with amazement at the sounds he could produce.

The boy's playing set the tone for the afternoon, and most of the kids opted to explore the sounds rather than just work on keeping a beat. The next player up was a young girl who was a little taller and could sit on the drum seat. She began, not by banging, but by testing the rhythmic waters, checking out the six cymbals and five drums in different combinations as her eyes shot back and forth from one instrument to another, associating the sound with the object.

An older boy was next, and he worked more on keeping a beat. He knew what he wanted to play and could hear it in his head, and he kept working at it until he was satisfied. His mother came in to hear him play later, and by then he had improved greatly.

The oldest boy in the group was next, and I could tell that he felt comfortable behind the set, especially since his legs could reach the pedals with no problems! He too worked on keeping time and exploring beats. Because he was the biggest kid in the group, I kind of expected him to tear into the kit and play louder than the others. Again, like the others, he was curious to hear what would happen when he hit a certain cymbal and drum combination.

After everyone had a chance to play, I took them over to a long table covered with various hand percussion instruments. They were very excited from having played, and they were equally curious about the inviting table. I encouraged them to pick up the instruments and play them to discover what they sounded like. Hands shot over hands – grabbing shakers, cowbells, woodblocks, whistles, tambourines... in twenty years of playing, I'd never seen a more excited bunch of musicians.

Next, I told them to grab their favorite percussion toy and follow me back to the drum set. I sat down behind the kit and told them that they were going to play along with me to experience working together as a group. I kept a simple but strong rock beat, and they locked right in.

I stopped and told them to play with their eyes closed to experience less distraction. Playing with your eyes closed gets you much more physically in touch with your instruments, which can have some very interesting effects on the player. I was trying to find ways to share some of the essentials of drumming with a beginner's group, and I think I succeeded on many counts.

After we finished playing, I asked them how they felt hearing applause for their individual performances. They liked it, a lot. I also asked them how it felt physically to play the drums and the percussion toys. One just said, "Cool." Another said it relaxed him, a few others said they enjoyed exploring the sounds. One of the girls said she felt embarrassed at first, but that feeling quickly left her as she began her exploration.

For the rest of the afternoon, I let anyone who wanted to come back up and play. Each of their performances and explorations went further than before, and I sat captivated at their individual processes. Twenty years of playing gives you a pretty good idea of what can be going through someone's head, and I felt like I was sharing in their private experiences.

What they *didn't* do was just beat the drums and go nuts. Each player wanted to see what she or he could do with the drums, and that was very inspiring. They were fresh minds exploring a sonic palette, finger-painting percussive soundscapes... and receiving applause from their peers.

To wrap the afternoon up, a few kids played for their parents. Most of them asked me to ask their folks to buy them a drum set. If I'd only had the money...

The hardships and brutal realities of living with Tourette Syndrome robs many a child of normal, pleasant growing experiences. Interest in activities comes and goes, and the idea of convincing a parent that drumming is not just another fad is a challenging one. However, I think that anyone who saw the kids play would agree on two things. First, the player's individual attention was totally locked into what they were doing, with absolute concentration and immediate experience. They were free to do whatever they wanted to, a rarely offered opportunity. Second, their tics disappeared as they played. I noticed a couple of boys in particular, sitting in their chairs (very patiently) exhibiting a fair amount of symptoms... until they played.

I've talked about this phenomenon for years, and it was fascinating to watch first-hand. When they sat down to play, I couldn't tell that any of them had a neurological disorder that would follow them the rest of their lives. They all said how much they enjoyed the chance to play, and I told them that if it were possible, I'd come back and they could do it some more. That put smiles on a quite a few faces, including mine.

After signing some books containing a story I'd written, I stopped to think about what had happened. For a couple of hours, TS kids had become "kid kids," playing and exploring in the truest sense and purest form of the words. My drums survived, with no busted heads or cracked cymbals. The percussion toys were okay too. In fact, the only thing broken that afternoon was silence and the walls of inhibition. I do believe we made some Tourette Syndrome history, and I hope for the sake of those kids and many others that what they say about history repeating itself is true.

You can count me in anytime.

/ /

We've covered what I believe are the important aspects of how music helped me deal with Tourette's during those undiagnosed years, and a few beyond. We can now move on and focus more specifically on the instruments I played and what I found appealing about them.

But before we do, let me offer just one word to summarize the essence of my fourteen-year search for an answer as to what caused my body to do what it was doing:

Relentless.

Music gave me the hope and the healing to keep going, to never stop looking, and to accept *nothing less* than discovering the absolute truth about what Tourette's was. As a result, I forged inner strength beyond anything I could have imagined, and I have drawn on it countless times.

Music was (and remains) the vehicle that taught me how to integrate all the parts of my life and express them in a way that made sense. Through the rough early years, music was a beacon, one that eventually led me to watching drummer Ed Shaughnessy on *The Tonight Show*, where I saw the public service announcement that led me to a correct diagnosis.

Simply put, music ultimately made me whole.

Now let's take a closer look at the individual tools that helped make it all happen...

Part II

The Instruments

Chapter 15

Acoustic and Electronic Drums

So far, we've talked mostly about the drums from the physical/ emotional perspective. In this chapter, we'll focus on what actually makes up an acoustic drum set, and then we'll briefly explore electronic drums to give you an idea of what you might need to get started with playing them.

A basic drum set consists of the following components: a snare drum with a band of wire strands stretched across the bottom head to give it a bright, cracking sound; a bass or kick drum, played with a foot pedal with a thick wooden, plastic, or felt beater to create a powerful impact; a ride cymbal, mounted on a stand, played with a drum stick to keep a timekeeping pulse; and a hi-hat, with two opposing cymbals mounted on a stand, moved up and down with a foot pedal.

Lastly, we have a padded drum seat that can be adjusted for height. The quality of the seat is definitely important, because physical discomfort behind the drum set interferes with both playing and the ability to relax. I use one with an adjustable back rest, but this is not absolutely necessary for a beginner.

Additional drums can be included in the core kit. Tom-toms are drums that are positioned above and around the bass drum on mounts, and floor toms are larger drums with supporting metal legs attached to their sides. Cymbals of varying sizes (with different associated sounds) can be combined to create many tonal possibilities. Crash cymbals ring brighter and longer than ride cymbals and are used to create a powerful emphasis, as opposed to a ride cymbal's timekeeping pulse.

In recent years, drum set manufacturers have produced kits designed for very young players. The sizes are smaller and more manageable for kids under the age of around nine, but they contain the same core pieces as a full-size kit. Smaller drum sticks are also available, putting the world of drumming that much sooner into the hands of future timekeepers.

But what do you do if you live in an apartment or have to face the reality that acoustic drums would disrupt the peace and quiet of everyone around you? In the early 1980's, an English company called Simmons introduced the first electronic drum set, and it changed the drumming game forever. Large plastic pads were mounted on stands just like an acoustic drum set. The pads had cables that ran into a sound module with volume controls, and when you struck the pad, it would send a signal to trigger a drum or cymbal sound in the module.

Many other electronic drum companies sprang up in the following years, refining the pads and sound modules, significantly expanding their capabilities. Today's kit pads are made of both solid rubber and even mesh surfaces that simulate a real drum head. The sound modules contain dozens of standard and custom drums sounds, and they let you modify and even create your own custom kits. The modules also contain electronic metronomes to help improve your timekeeping abilities, something I definitely benefited from.

Another feature of many electronic drum kits are song and recording capabilities; they include a library of pre-recorded songs that you can play along to, and many also allow you to record your own drumming. You can hear yourself play either through a headset or an external amplifier, and if you choose the headset option, the kit only makes a muffled tapping sound as the sticks hit the rubber pads.

Most music stores have kits set up for you to try out, and they are reasonably priced. You can also buy used kits and get started for a fairly low cost. As you progress in your playing, you can buy upgraded sound modules and add more pads.

An electronic kit will never replace the sound or feel of an acoustic kit, but it's a great alternative if loud noises are going to create problems at home. It's a perfect compromise: players get music, listeners get relative peace.

I use both kinds of kits; the acoustic is mostly for live performance, and the electronic is for home recording. With either kit choice, the first time your sit down behind one will be a moment that can transform you *and* provide access to a very socially acceptable form of movement.

It's a percussive win-win!

Tourette Syndrome and Music

Chapter 16

Piano and Synthesizer

My brother Charlie expressed an interest in learning piano when we were both in high school, and my mom purchased a small Baldwin upright (which Charlie still has). I was taking a music theory class in high school, and having a piano helped me make great sense of something I'd have otherwise had little or no way to relate to.

As mentioned in previous chapters, my attention deficit prevented me from being able to learn how to read music very well, but I quickly discovered that I could play by ear. It had been many years since I'd played a piano, but the attraction to something so physical and tonal was an immediate draw.

I would sit at the keyboard, pecking out notes and stretching my hands to make chords by playing multiple notes at a time. Just as I did in kindergarten, I'd often rest my ear against the piano and close my eyes, gently touching the ivory keys and drinking in their vibration as the felt pads struck the thin wires within the sound board.

Pressing the sustain pedal with my foot would let the notes ring without dampening them, and this was a source of enormous pleasure. The fine motor movement involved with using my fingers helped me focus and concentrate better as well. The right combination of notes would produce minor chords, or sad and haunting tones, and they in turn produced a very physical tingling effect. I spent hours figuring out how to construct chords that not only sounded nice but made me feel a certain way.

Trying to learn how to read piano music was difficult, but I did give it a shot. It took forever to remember what the symbols for sharps and flats meant, and I finally surrendered to the fact that I was not likely ever going to be able to do this with much ease. I instead focused on learning how to improvise on the piano. I'd take a simple melody and try to create sounds like it, remembering where to place my fingers on the keys to produce the desired results. I had limited success, but it was fun nonetheless.

During this time, I wrote a few simple compositions, listening to whatever musical notes popped into my head and working to recreate them on the keyboard. I'd hoped to develop the kind of flow of consciousness I had with drumming, but there was much more work involved.

Still, even with the simple songs, the physical pleasure and release of pressing against the keys was a wonderful feeling. It connected me heart and soul, whereas with normal living, I was always trying to get *away* from my body, and escape into my thoughts.

However, the pleasure derived from "being present" and concentrating on producing a sound was something quite different. In the privacy of our basement, I could melt into the notes and feel no fear, no pain, and be free from insults and hurtful teasing. This was priceless pleasure.

/ /

The percussive nature of the piano lent itself to letting me pound the keys at times, and from these raw exercises, I eventually developed enough control in my fingers to play brief, rapid patterns that relieved lots of stress and sounded good as well. The releasing of positive energy was probably the best result, as I moved fingers over the keys that felt solid and smooth. It was a very pleasant, tactile sensation.

This is what much of Tourette's is all about, and anything that makes you feel good is something you'll likely spend time going after. To this day, I still enjoy the sensation of playing weighted keys on a piano. There's something very soothing about pressing down on them and creating vibrations that resonate through my entire body. If you ever try it, you'll instantly know what I mean.

I never learned how to read piano music well enough to sight read or even play a rehearsed piece, but my limited skills were good enough to get me through a live performance as a piano player at the last jazz band performance of my senior year. I'd been practicing two pieces I'd written, and one was for my girlfriend. Her song had seven beats to the measure, and it was the kind of odd meter exploration I was really enjoying at the time. The other tune had five beats to the measure, and it was a little faster than the first.

Long story short: I walked out onto the stage alone after having played an intense drum solo in the song "Quiet Friday" (that I talked about in "Rhythm Man"). I sat down at the black grand piano and could barely see the audience beyond the bright white stage lights. I took a breath, lowered my hands to the ivory keys, and began to play…

The intensity of the moment was unlike anything I'd ever experienced. Playing a blazing drum solo was one thing; having complete control and say over the tempo and pace of a solo piano performance was quite another. My fingers seemed to move on their own, and I listened closely to every note that left the sound board and filled the auditorium.

There was a real moment of musical truth halfway through the first song, where just for a second, I *forgot* where my fingers needed to go next. It took my breath away, but I focused, gently put my fingers on the keys, and pressed down, hoping I'd found the right notes. Talk about a leap of performance faith! No nervous tics to be found anywhere, either; this was one-hundred percent concentration, and Tourette's would not interrupt this night.

Fortunately, I *did* find the right notes. I also remembered to breathe, and I went on to the next song without any mistakes. When I hit the last note and let it ring, the audience let loose with shrill whistles and applause the likes of which I'd never known. So, for a few moments on that special evening, I was also a piano player, and not too bad a one.

Today, you can buy acoustic pianos (and less expensive electric pianos) that literally teach you how to play. The keyboard can be configured to move with the notes, with sheet music in front of you on a computer screen showing you where to put your fingers. If I'd had something like that as a kid, there's no telling how much it would have helped. I suspect it would have been quite a lot.

/ /

That said, how does playing a synthesizer compare to its acoustic counterpart? It's a little different in terms of the physical touch, and the sounds that are possible are incredible. It can be technically overwhelming at first, because there are many knobs, buttons, and keys to adjust and create sounds with. The best way to proceed is to go with the default settings, learn how to load the basic sounds, and explore from there.

The instruction manuals can seem dense at first, so you need to take your time studying the simple set-up guidelines. From there, you just start pressing keys. The string and horn sounds are incredibly realistic, and the custom synth sounds are out of this world. Once you can hear them in your head and think in terms of them, you develop an entirely new vocabulary that expands you as a musician.

Tourette Syndrome and Music

I remember very clearly sitting in a high school auditorium one day with our music class, listening to a demonstration by a representative from ARP, a synthesizer manufacturer from Massachusetts. He really blew us away with his performance, and I'll never forget his closing and prophetic words:

"This is the instrument of the future."

Our high school band director convinced the powers that be to purchase one, allowing our jazz ensemble to really step into the exploration with both feet. About ten years later, I was living in Santa Cruz, California, and I attended a demonstration by a Yamaha representative who showed us how one keyboard could drive sounds in several other keyboards using a technology called MIDI.

Musical Instrument Digital Interface was the most incredible thing I'd ever seen or heard in terms of music composition potential. Why? Because not only could you play sounds on multiple keyboards all from one keyboard, but you could also record what you played into a computer, and then play it back.

You could edit the sounds, and you could record and place passages of songs anywhere you wanted in a song, just like cutting and pasting text in a word processor file.

For someone with ADD, let me tell you, *this* was gold.

And while I never did learn how to fully play/read piano music, it doesn't matter as much now, because MIDI also lets me play and have the software write out the sheet music *for* me, in real time. Simply amazing.

Tourette Syndrome and Music

Aside from the potential for composition exploration, synthesizers let me create many unusual tonal textures. People with Tourette's have a heightened sense of touch and sensation, so, playing a synthesizer lets me go places with vibration and sensation that an acoustic piano never could.

During that Yamaha demo, the representative also linked a synthesizer to several rack-mounted sound modules containing all the sounds of the main synthesizer, minus the additional keyboards. He then sent all those sounds into a computer to record and edit, where he performed and recorded the theme from "48 Hours" on the spot for us. The future had arrived.

For any parents reading this book, an investment in a simple MIDI keyboard set-up with a modest synthesizer could prove to be a very valuable and therapeutic tool for your child. Also, much of the technology is linkable to smart tablets and smart phones, allowing them to compose music on them and then export it to more complex sound sources.

Whether you choose to explore acoustic piano or synthesizer, lessons for both can be very helpful… but may I suggest first letting your kids play in the truest sense and enjoy that personal freedom. Take them to a music store sometime and see for yourself. And remember, while not everyone has to become, nor will become a professional musician, they can benefit so very much from the simple experience of free musical exploration.

Chapter 17

Acoustic Guitar, Electric Guitar, and Bass Guitar

One of my cherished family heirlooms is my paternal grandmother's acoustic guitar. It was the first stringed instrument I ever laid my hands on, and I can still remember what those steel strings felt like. The 1930's-era Slingerland *Songster* is a brown, hollow-body wooden guitar that I used to love watching my grandmother bring out and play. I was six years old, with small hands, so it was a challenge to actually form a chord, but she was very patient and encouraging.

I would stretch my left hand and fingers around the guitar's neck and try to press all the strings down without making them buzz. When I got it right, the strumming of the strings with the right hand would produce simple but beautiful sounds. I'd put my ear against the body of the guitar and feel the vibrations, just playing and listening with my eyes closed, pleasantly drifting away from the nervous movements of my young body. Playing it today brings back very fond memories.

As mentioned earlier, my mom bought me a smaller acoustic guitar and enrolled me in a local music store for private lessons. If you (or if you are a parent, your child) are interested in learning the guitar this way, explain to the instructor what Tourette's is, and they'll work to help you discover the instrument.

For kids under twelve or so, small-sized acoustic guitars are now available, with either steel or nylon strings. The nylon ones are quieter and softer on the fingers. Strings are strummed with small plastic teardrop-shaped discs called picks, to help isolate individual strings. The fine motor control required to hold a pick might be a little much for some beginning students, but with practice, you do become more comfortable at holding a pick and strumming with it.

I used a simple instruction book with pictures of guitar chords when I first started. There were photographs of hands as well as diagrams of guitar necks with dots where you would put your fingers. Both of these teaching tools helped me learn how to build simple chords. Today there are many DVD instruction options available, along with software programs and apps ranging from simple to very complex. YouTube has literally thousands of posts as well, covering as wide a range as you could imagine regarding guitar instruction.

From a touch point of view, playing acoustic guitar will cause small callouses to build up on the fingertips forming the chord. It takes a little time, but they develop fairly quickly with regular practice, and they make it easier to play overall.

/ /

I first picked up the electric guitar when I was thirteen, the one I mentioned that my maternal grandmother bought me.

Tourette Syndrome and Music

I kept it for awhile, and I was able to remember the basic chords I'd learned as a kid. It was fun to plug it into the little practice amp and be a rock star for an afternoon. I had a good musical ear and could pick out tunes pretty quickly.

Thanks to the incredibly successful "Guitar Hero" and "Rock Star," you can also explore the instrument without strings, to develop the hand coordination necessary to pick out notes. It's a beneficial option in many ways. I played my acoustic guitar for a few months but lost interest in it, mostly because the metal strings hurt my fingers. The nice thing about the "simulated" guitars is that there's no pain at all.

Today, I have an electric guitar in my home studio that I can play and transmit sounds from directly into my computer recording equipment. I still enjoy playing simple chords, closing my eyes and remembering the earliest tones and vibrations that lead me towards the musical path. There's also something soothing about the smooth feel of a solid wood guitar neck that makes the experience additionally pleasing.

The finger movements without a pick connect me even more directly to the instrument and to the sounds being produced. If I can hear the sounds in my head and sing them, my fingers can usually find where they need to go on the guitar neck to make those sounds, and that's still a great creative release.

The last stringed instrument I'll share experiences about is the electric bass guitar. I began learning how to play it in ninth grade, because I was attracted to the dense and throbbing low frequencies it generated. The four large strings were easier to play, and the instrument in general seemed less complicated. Also, I could easily see where the note positions for the fingers were on the bass guitar neck.

I bought an imitation Fender Precision bass, along with an inexpensive bass guitar amp to get started. This electric combination was the source of many hours of fun, especially coming home directly after school. I'd crank up Pink Floyd's "Dark Side of the Moon," and my little amp did a good job of pumping out the volume as well. In the days before "Rock Star," it was fun to play along to real records, even if it meant fumbling all over the place. I developed a pretty good ear for playing the bass, and I was able to pick out the notes to make basic songs work.

The bass guitar is an important instrument; it's what holds music and rhythm together, and if you listen to jazz or funk, you will find there are players who can do some amazing things with four strings. Advanced bass players use basses that have 5, 6 and 7 strings, and that's a handful! Run the instrument through a stack of amps, and your chest will thump like a floored muscle car from the palpitations.

When you first start to play with other musicians, you must learn to listen *very* closely to everything that's going on. The bass guitar, in many ways, becomes the center of the song. It's not as glamorous an instrument as say, the lead guitar, but it is definitely a needed one. Without it, there is no tonal bottom end, and there is no driving musical pulse. The next time you hear a song you like, listen to the bass guitar and how it creates the common musical theme with simple notes.

If you develop some ability on it, you'll become a sought-after player. I never played bass full-time in a band, but I did have the opportunity to sit in with bands every once in a while and be something other than a drummer. Doing so really opened my eyes as to how a drummer needs to behave and interact with other musicians to help make good music.

As a drummer, I was guilty many times of trampling all over a song in the name of self-indulgence. Whatever the instrument you play, maturity must grow side-by-side with talent. Playing all the guitar family instruments helped me understand the value of that lesson and grow as a musician.

I only played bass guitar in public a couple of times, and once was at the same final high school jazz band performance in 1977 where I had the drum solo in "Quiet Friday" and where I played solo piano. My core musician friends played a Billy Cobham tune called "Red Baron," with myself on bass, Jim Shepherd on drums, Paul Harlyn on synthesizer, and Mark Wallace on electric guitar. Playing the bass that night was serious musical fun!

All of the guitar-family instruments we've discussed help develop and improve fine-motor control. It does require a little work, but if you take your time and keep your practice sessions short and simple, you will continue to improve each time you play. Like the electric and acoustic guitar, smaller-sized versions of bass guitars are available for children.

I'd say that next to drumming, the electric bass is probably the instrument I could most likely transition to full-time. When I record my own tunes today in my home studio, I truly enjoy creating and playing my own bass guitar parts.

It has the essential element of rhythm, and it also lets you anchor the entire band from a tonal perspective. It's a very important linking instrument in this sense, and while it doesn't always make you the star of the show, you can be sure that to your fellow musicians, you *are* the rhythmic and harmonic glue that holds the band together.

And if you really want to hear where this instrument can go, check out Jaco Pastorius...

Part III

The Inner Workings

Chapter 18

Drumming and Four-Limb Coordination Secrets Revealed

Now that we've talked a bit about the instruments I've explored and benefitted from, I'll share some information about how playing the drums actually works from the inside out. I've mentioned how the four-limb coordination I acquired from playing the drum set helped me control my case of Tourette's, but what does it really mean, and how does it happen?

I believe the answer can be presented in a way that will make sense, and we'll explore a few playing exercises to give you a taste of what drumming and four-limb coordination is really all about.

When I first sat down behind Ken Berry's drum set way back in fourth grade, he let me just play and explore. After I figured out how to keep my balance while moving my hands and feet, Ken gave me a very simple beat to play. The first thing he had me do was tap single notes on the big cymbal to my right, called a ride cymbal. It's the thick one that makes a "ping" sound when you play it.

Ken counted out "1-2-3-4" and had me play just those single notes. Then, he had me count out loud and play. That was my first experience with coordination, doing two things at once. Ken was trying to get me to synchronize my mind with my body. For years, I'd run away from my body; now I was willingly turning inward... which was strange...

Ken had me play evenly spaced notes and count out loud equally so I wouldn't speed up or slow down. Next, he had me play the bass drum, using the same notes as my hands. I was trying to do *three* things at once: play my right hand, my right foot, and count out loud. This was a real challenge!

Then he had me add my left hand to play the snare drum only on beats "2" and "4" while remaining silent on beats "1" and "3." It felt even stranger trying to do *four* things at once, but I was actually playing a simple rock beat, and it didn't sound too bad.

Now let's try that same exercise now with a basic drumming lesson of your own...

Start by counting the numbers "1-2-3-4" out loud, evenly. Repeat this four times.

"1-2-3-4"

"1-2-3-4"

"1-2-3-4"

"1-2-3-4"

Okay, tap your **right** hand on your **right** leg at the same time you are counting the numbers "1-2-3-4" out loud.

Next, tap your **right** foot and your **right** hand, at the same time, counting "1-2-3-4" out loud.

All right... *now,* tap your **right** hand and **right** foot <u>without</u> counting out loud.

A little different, isn't it? Don't be surprised if you hear you voice counting the numbers in your head. This process is called *audiation*, and it's pretty cool to use as a mental practice tool. Invaluable, actually.

Finally, let's add something to the mix by including your **left** hand. Play the pattern you've just practiced, and see if you can play your **left** hand on only beats "2" and "4."

Now, try this while counting out loud, "1-2-3-4."

Interesting, eh?

So, this gives you a little taste of what drummers first learn in formal lessons. You'll improve with more practice.

Now I'm going to share with you the secret to playing two things at once: you HEAR and FEEL them as ONE SOUND.

Try the **right** hand and **left** hand again, and refer to the diagram below. Play it slowly, and on beats "2" and "4," really feel BOTH hands striking your legs at exactly the same time.

Count	1 2 3 4
Right hand	/ / / /
Left hand	/ /

Try this four times. Then, try it with your eyes closed, paying very close attention to the sensation of your hands hitting your legs AND hearing the sounds they produce.

This is how you become a drummer. It's also how I still practice: by feeling and hearing. I pay close attention to the movement of my hands and feet going up and down in between striking a surface, to feel and remain aware of the silence and the space. Doing this keeps my concentration always present, as opposed to dropping off in between the notes.

Of course, it took many years of practice to develop control of my hands and of my feet to make the rhythm patterns and timekeeping flow, but everything you've just experienced in these exercises is exactly what I feel when I play.

Now, let me tell you about where I was able to take it…

/ /

When I studied jazz with Mr. Kenny at The Percussion Center, he taught me how to keep time by playing a jazz beat. It took some work, but he actually got me to use all four limbs doing different things at once, or at least, it sounded that way. Again, I want to keep this explanation simple, but the bottom line is that four-way coordination is really kind of a sound illusion, as the mind can actually only focus consciously on one thing at a time.

So, to conceive of multiple sounds at once, I focused on hearing **two sounds** as one sound, and then **three sounds** as one sound. I then put these group movements on a sort of "rhythmic autopilot" and repeated them while adding new sounds with one hand or one foot. Lastly, I would hear all four sounds as one, single event. And that's kinda tricky...

Tourette Syndrome and Music

Mr. Kenny's advice about hearing multiple events as a single event reminded me of a listening lesson we had way back in third grade, in Austin, Texas. Our teacher, Miss Britton, played two records with two different conversations going on. She was teaching us how to isolate and focus on one voice at a time, which was a really cool thing to learn!

I doubt she thought the idea of selective listening would ever be applied by one of her students for use in the music world, but I'm sure glad she played those conversations that day. My ears and mind received a most interesting re-wiring as a result.

/ /

This kind of listening is *exactly* what goes on while you are keeping a beat with a band. You listen to what you're doing and to what everyone else is playing, and you also listen to how loud you are playing each drum and cymbal. A drummer is also expected to be their own sound mixer, balancing out the individual volumes of each limb.

Talk about multi-tasking!

Okay, so you have all this going on... *and*, you are expected to anticipate what the other musicians are going to do if everyone is improvising. The whole affair becomes very much like living with Tourette's; you don't know what's going to happen next, but you know that *something* is going to happen, so, you listen very closely and prepare to adapt and improvise around whatever the other musicians play.

The combination of listening and controlling both the coordination and the volume levels of your individual limbs cannot help but give you some aid in managing your mind and body. It surely did in my case, and, in many ways, I am only just beginning to truly understand and more deeply appreciate this unity.

/ /

Playing drums can involve anything from heavy metal pounding to whisper-quiet jazz brushwork. Regardless of which path you chose, you develop a broad span of physical and mental awareness, which is what can lead to more overall control. It takes time and work, but the investment of both is invaluable if you can benefit in any way.

And the best part? It's incredibly fun!

Chapter 19

Ever Forward

I thought it might be informative to share one final look at how I play the drums today. It's no longer simply the rabid unleashing of teen angst and raging frustration. Many decades have passed since then, and I now sit down behind the drum kit with a deeper respect for tradition, my role as a team member, and my freedom and responsibility as a creative artist.

Sometimes when I practice, I play the simplest beat I can create, just to focus on keeping time. I listen to the sound of each instrument (each individual drum and cymbal), and I strive to produce a definitive tone with every strike. Doing this keeps me very "present" in what I'm doing and with what's happening.

I really enjoy working with the subtle aspects of playing jazz, maintaining my touch with quiet and fast timekeeping, then back to slow and quiet. I often work with brushes to refine my touch, and I find this to be very relaxing.

I also do a standard warm-up using medium, heavy and lightweight sticks, playing loud, medium and soft volumes back and forth to keep my hands flexible and my ears alert. The speed is still there, and I do love letting that wild animal out of its cage, although nowadays, I control it far better than I ever could before. It has its place in certain types of music, and in growing as a musician, I've focused less on it... but I have to admit, there's still *nothing* quite like firing up the energy machine and letting it run off the leash!

In the past few years, I've also explored singing and drumming, doing beat boxing, where you imitate the sounds. It's a lot fun, and a great way to practice keeping the connection between mind and body very strong. Often, I'll sing the patterns into my phone or a digital recorder and then go back and work with them later on the drum set.

This is especially helpful when I am creating really fast and complex pattern ideas. They don't get lost, and I can keep the neural pathways primed as well. I suppose as our world advances, I've been sucked into the multimedia, multi-tasking thinking, but in a way, Tourette's is the perfect tool to be wired with for this pursuit.

The vocalizing of rhythm patterns is something I've refined to a level where I can sing almost as fast as I can play. I also practice generating the sounds in my head, just like being able to hear yourself think. This process is called *audiation*, and it really is an amazing way to integrate the senses to re-enforce a complete mind/body performance.

Loire Cotler, the artist and music therapist who graciously provided the foreword to this book, has significantly influenced my exploration of singing rhythm patterns. Loire incorporates South Indian drumming syllables from a centuries' old system known as *konnakol*, and I have borrowed from her techniques to generate my own vocabulary of drumming sounds to explore. Calling her extraordinary is an understatement, and I encourage anyone who is curious about singing and drumming to learn more about Loire Cotler and her work with renowned frame drummer Glen Velez at www.loirevox.com.

I also very much enjoy rediscovering the roots of modern jazz by playing bebop, the fast-paced small group music from the late 40's and 50's. This period was a real explosion in terms of changing the direction of jazz, and I want to see if I can find ways to blend the old school with new technology.

/ /

Music never moved an inch forward by players holding back, and I have many more paths to explore, particularly with odd meters and polyrhythms. There are so many possible areas to pursue that sometimes it's a little overwhelming, but in the end, drumming continues to be the most amazing journey I have ever been on, and I cherish my time behind the kit now more than ever.

I love showing kids how much fun the world of music can be, and I hope to spend many more years demonstrating the drums, hand percussion, and perhaps even the other musical instruments I play. I want every young person with Tourette's I meet to know just how much magic is at their fingertips, and I want them to know that there are many options for exploring that magic. I think of it as being of musical service, and it's something that I'm very proud to be involved with.

For the most part though, drumming remains very much a therapeutic pursuit, providing relief from stress, although the levels have dropped considerably over the years. I've also gained a very different and more mature perspective of playing, wanting to honor the greats who have come before me by keeping their exploring spirit alive and not simply falling into the rut of literally playing it safe.

Certainly, one aspect of my drumming has remained constant over the years, and I doubt it will ever change. When I sit down behind a kit in front of an audience, I feel a little nervous and unsure for a second, wondering how things will turn out. But once the music starts and I leap, the fears fall away, the steeled confidence emerges, and there is no question as to which way the wagon is going to roll: ever forward.

I'd like to close out our discussion of drumming and the playing experience by describing what goes through my mind when I perform. Specifically, I'd like to tell you about what it's like to walk into a club and sit in with complete strangers. No rehearsal, just walk into an open "jam" session where you make up a great deal of it all on the spot.

There is nothing quite like live improvisation to test your mental and musical abilities, and I love experiencing this kind of performance. If Tourette Syndrome was ever meant to be tapped into and drawn from, this is the perfect environment (at least for me) for turning a disability into an ability. You really do sink or swim, but you don't drown. You just get wet, go home, practice, and get better at doing *this*...

/ /

It's a Wednesday night at a local club where they are having an open jazz playing opportunity. I sign my name on a play sheet and wait to be called up. Several musicians are on the stage already; a piano player, bass guitar player, saxophone and trumpet player, and a guitarist. The leader, often the piano player, calls out a standard jazz tune. We are either already familiar with it, or, we read the music out of something called a "Fake book," with chord outlines and the basic melody.

Drummers usually just keep time, but if they own a Fake book, they can follow the printed music. Let's say it's a tune I'm unfamiliar with; I ask the leader to briefly describe the song's structure, and I will fill in everything as I go along.

I sit down behind the unfamiliar drum set and make small adjustments, like changing the angle of a cymbal or the tension of the snare drum head. I ensure all my drum sticks, brushes, and mallets are easily within reach, I adjust the seat once more, and then I lock eyes with the band leader.

The song tempo is counted off, and I start playing a simple pulse on the big ride cymbal, not too loud, matching the tempo the band leader set, while listening extremely closely to the bass player's notes. The bass guitar can sometimes play exactly on the beat, a millisecond behind, or a millisecond ahead. My job is to figure out where this timing is in relation to the time that was counted off.

That's critical, because *this* is how the rhythm section creates forward movement and tension. If the drummer lays back, and the bass player is pushing, it creates an interesting pull-push feel that the other band members use to play in between. This tension concept is used in all musical styles, and it's what makes things sound and feel the way they do.

So, in a just a few seconds, I have to solve the time placement issue and then immediately balance out my own sounds. Remember, I'm playing four instruments at once (snare, bass drum, ride cymbal, and hi-hat). Each of these instruments has to have *just* the right amount of volume, and the overall balance has to mix well with the rest of the band. This adjustment is made quickly and is then fine-tuned.

As the song progresses, I also am responsible for keeping the energy going. I can't just sit and listen as though I am in the audience simply enjoying the music, because the fact is, I AM the music, or at least a part of the whole. I keep it all energized by constantly tuning in to the individual instruments and adding rhythmic punctuations using the snare drum, bass drum, tom-toms, and cymbals.

Next, I have to figure out where the song is going, as all songs have some sort of form. When someone is taking a solo,

Tourette Syndrome and Music

I have to provide solid timekeeping for them to build their music upon, and I am also listening to the other instruments as they make short statements of their own. I build on these statements by either repeating their rhythmic structure or by varying their theme using different drums and cymbals.

The trick is to make it all sound *just* recognizable enough to fit and support the music. It's also a fun mental exercise to keep track of all the little bits and pieces that the individual musicians create and then put them back together in my own performance mosaic. This is one of my favorite aspects of playing jazz, because no two versions of a song ever sound exactly alike... nor should they.

All of this is going on second-by-second, and there must be a balance between listening and participating. If you lean towards one perspective more than other, the musical equation is incomplete. Listen too much and you miss out on energizing the music; play without listening, and you miss subtle cues that reinforce time and flow.

The song is moving along, musicians are soloing, and I'm constantly watching the leader and all the other players to deeply interact with them and to catch very slight but important signals when something new is about to happen. I listen closely for transitions from one part of a song to another, and I do what I can to make the shifts as smooth as possible. This means knowing when to push and play a little bit more, or maybe lay back and play a little less. It's rarely the same way twice, so, you can't expect things to just fall into place with no effort. In other words, you are always THERE.

Some soloists need and like a lot of activity from the drummer, while others do not. I must determine this expectation within a few notes and not stray from the role I must provide. Experience tells me what the musicians likely expect, and the important thing is to NOT get in their way. A drummer will stay employed forever if they leave *lots* of room for the other musicians to play and create within.

/ /

Finally, it's my turn, and I get to play some solo drumming. The band will move towards a musical transition, and then they go silent. I now fill in my own interpretation of musical ideas. Sometimes the bass player may continue, and I will solo over whatever repeated tonal pattern is being played.

In either case, I work to restate musical ideas that remind the listener of the overall song, and this is where learning about tonal music becomes crucial for any serious drummer. It's called *music*-making, not drum smack-making. Jazz drummers in particular are expected to have a heightened awareness of song form so that when it comes time for them to solo, they can contribute to the overall essence of the tune just like every other player. It requires a high degree of focus, composure, and a lot of finesse.

Tourette Syndrome and Music

Sometimes, I first hear what I'm going to play in my head; other times, I just play as though I am speaking. The coolest times are when the sounds coming out of my hands and feet are being produced on the spot, simply by moving. I hear the sounds, feel the impact of the sticks and pedals, and they become my new vocabulary. However it is accomplished, the process and the experience of playing is simply amazing, and the freer I allow it to become, the purer and more fascinating it becomes.

I use varying volumes levels, creating basic musical statements that I will then modify and restate on different drums and cymbals. I use accents, fast patterns, slow patterns, whatever comes to mind to add to the flavor of the song. I work to keep my musical statements simple and consistent, not insane and rambling. I want to compose, not just hit things, and doing this in the "now" is very cool!

When my solo is just about over, I make visual contact with the leader, and the other band members get ready to start playing again. As the whole band rejoins, the music's energy surges, the basic tune is replayed, and then it gets wrapped up.

If I did my job right, the other musicians will likely just nod and smile. Sometimes that's all you need to let you know that you did your part well and did not overplay or make things too complicated. Music was created, ideas were exchanged, and art once again came to life.

That's what it's really all about.

Part IV

The Outcome

Tourette Syndrome and Music

Chapter 20

The True Musical Highlights

So what has a lifetime of moving in and out of music ultimately yielded? Maybe not all that I'd hoped for, but certainly more than I expected...

Over the last thirty-five years, I've lived and played music in Los Angeles and Santa Cruz, California, and also in Austin, Texas. Some of the more interesting and colorful musicians I worked with include bassist Paul Lamb and Opus One, a progressive Los Angeles rock group with some garage band thrown in; Santa Cruz 7-string guitarist Bob Burnett, who along with bassist Rhan Wilson, helped me bring odd meter funk to life with our group, Tuesday Night Leather.

There was guitarist Dirk Price, whom I first met in Austin in the 80's, whose School Without Walls through the Dick Grove School of Music offers incredible distance learning music education opportunities (www.dickgrove.com); Kathy Murray and her band, the Kilowatts, who patiently taught me the truth about playing a Texas shuffle; the late and tornado-intense guitarist Nicky Shoes, who along with bassist Sammy Persons, who gave me the most intense electric blues experiences of my life playing in Los Angeles.

And last but surely not least, honky-tonk piano player Will "Old Jake" Jacobs (www.reverbnation.com/willjacobs), who along with The O'Neal Brothers (an Austin, Texas, country/ Western band) taught me to respect musical authenticity in whatever form the cows brought back to the barn. And truthfully, we did play in more than one barn...

But if we want to talk *real* highlights, moving to California gave me the opportunity to do something I could have never imagined possible growing up in Delaware: when I was 20, I auditioned for Frank Zappa, the man who redefined intelligence and complexity in rock music.

I had met his drummer, Vinnie Colaiuta, in a local L.A. bar called *The Baked Potato*, and we struck up a conversation. We became friends, and soon after, he asked me if I was interested in giving Frank Zappa's band a shot. I hovered around my phone for two weeks waiting for the call from Vinnie to drive over to Zappa's North Hollywood rehearsal warehouse.

Finally, it rang...

This would be a *tough* audition. It seemed like every drummer in town was going for the position. Zappa's music was extremely demanding, containing a lot of odd meter structures. Luckily, I had been exposed to plenty of them through Hank Levy's music. Once I got to the warehouse, I introduced myself at the front desk, and a few minutes later I was told to walk through the door into the back room where the very loud music was coming from. The butterflies in my stomach were screaming at the top of their fluttering lungs, but I stayed focused and introduced myself to the man himself.

Tourette Syndrome and Music

I sat down behind a massive, double-bass drum set-up with a vast array of cymbals and tom-toms. Zappa described what he wanted me to play, and I asked him if I could write down the basic structure. He didn't mind, so I scribbled it as fast as I could. For musicians reading this, the meter was 13/8, subdivided 4/4 + 5/8, with a 12/8 bridge, then repeat...

Arthur Barrow was playing bass, and he was the guy who led the rehearsals most of the time when Zappa was away. Arthur told me to "Just keep time," so keep time I did, playing as solid a beat as I could figure out. The music was very complex, but I was able to keep up with it fairly well for about fifteen minutes. However, when Zappa asked me if I could play reggae in 13/8, I knew I'd met my match!

He thanked me for coming in, shook my hand, and I left feeling like I'd entered another world. And actually, I had. For those few minutes, I'd left Tourette Syndrome far behind and gone directly to the head of the music class.

/ /

Two years later, I had another musical highlight, this time in my hometown of Austin, Texas. It was with a rock singer from England who was very famous, and for whom both Frank Zappa and Jimi Hendrix had opened shows. Arthur Brown was already something of a rock legend, having influenced David Bowie, Peter Gabriel, and Alice Cooper, and his 1968 worldwide hit, "Fire," had put him on the charts straight to the top and cemented his status into the rock history books.

Arthur had moved to Austin to explore the growing music scene of the 1980's. Word spread that he was looking for a drummer, and somehow my name had gotten to him. Tommy Robertson, owner of Tommy's Drum Shop (the most awesome drum shop on the planet!), told me about Arthur one day when I walked in for my usual morning of hanging out and banging on things. Tommy was a real saint, because he'd let me come in after downing some soda and Twinkies and go nuts on any surface designed for hitting with a drumstick.

Seriously, a saint, I tell you.

I was 22 and had just moved back from Los Angeles to decompress for a while. I also wanted to spend some time in Austin living with my dad, hopefully to get to know him a little better after a rough, thirteen-year, long-distance relationship. Hearing that Arthur Brown wanted to check me out was pretty surreal, and just another strange leg on an increasingly interesting musical journey.

My Tourette's was fairly intense mentally, and it gave me endless amounts of energy, and this was exactly what Arthur Brown wanted from his musicians. I was told he liked his drummers to play *very* loud, so I borrowed a large, green Ludwig marching snare from Tommy Robertson to take to the audition. I also stopped by a local drug store to pick up some swimmer's ear wax as decibel protection.

Tourette Syndrome and Music

I'd already met with Arthur's keyboard player, Daniel McCloud, who'd walked me through the songs to get a feel for them. I memorized the cassette tape he gave me and showed up a week later at a funky rehearsal hall in South Austin. Arthur was a tall, lanky Englishman with a deep, resonant baritone voice that could also hit octaves in the stratosphere. A few measures into the first tune, with me smashing the drums with everything I had, I saw a big smile on Arthur's face.

This time, I *got* the job!

I went on to record a demo tape with Arthur, but it didn't get picked up by the studios, so a few months later, I returned to California. Arthur had landed another deal by then, and I got to play on three tracks of this mostly electronic percussion-driven album called *Requiem* (Republic Records). And in a very small world of musical irony, one of the other musicians on the album was Frank Zappa's bass player, Arthur Barrow, the guy I played the Zappa audition with.

Go figure.

Ten years later, *Requiem* was re-released on CD, and it included the demo tracks we'd recorded in Austin. One of the songs off of *Requiem,* called "Busha-Busha," was made into a video that aired on MTV. You can view it on YouTube by doing a search for the song title. I'm not physically in the video, but that's my drumming, pounding away in the background!

Another significant accomplishment occurred in Austin around that same time, when I had the opportunity to play drums in front of jazz legend Max Roach, who had worked with be-bop masters Charlie Parker and Clifford Brown. Max was conducting a drum clinic at Tommy's Drum Shop, and he demonstrated the use of different volume levels to add dimension and content to his performance. I studied him carefully, knowing this would probably be one of the rare chances I would ever have to sit at the feet of a true jazz master and soak in some truth.

Max then asked drummers from the audience to come play. When it was my turn, I got up and tried to recreate some of the themes Max had played and then improvised on them. Later, I brought one of Max's records over for him to sign. He shook my hand, and as he was writing, Max smiled and said, "That was some complex stuff you were playing."

You could have knocked me over with a feather.

/ /

In May 1988, a true drumming dream came to life when I was included in a feature interview in *Modern Drummer* magazine (issue #100). "Beating Drums, Beating Disabilities" was written by my friend and writing mentor, the late Adam Ward Seligman. He interviewed me for the piece and let me describe the relationship between Tourette's and drumming. It was an incredible honor to make it into *Modern Drummer*, and it was really the start of my wanting to share thoughts on how drumming served as therapy. In fact, it was this article that inspired me to eventually write "Rhythm Man" for Adam when he was co-editing *Don't Think About Monkeys.*

Certainly one very unexpected music-related highlight was my becoming a features writer for *DRUM!* magazine. I wrote for them from 1992-2002, and thanks to editor Andy Doershuck, I was given some amazing opportunities to meet and interview many of the world's top drummers. Believe me, this was something I *never* expected to ever be doing when I dreaming of a music career as a kid.

Perhaps the longest-lasting musical highlight was having the opportunity to study with one of Frank Zappa's drummers when I lived in Los Angeles. The ripple effect of that study period altered the course of my life for the next thirty years, and I suppose it's a good place to wind things down.

In the fall of 1981, I answered an ad placed by Terry Bozzio in a local music magazine, offering drum set instruction. I leapt at the chance to study with him, hoping I might someday go back and successfully re-audition for Frank Zappa. During those lessons, Bozzio showed me a handful of rhythm patterns that he said were the basic elements of all larger rhythm patterns... and this was pure gold.

I immediately saw an application for the study of these patterns, and I began writing out an initial list of possible rhythm pattern combinations, and in the process, I discovered just how much of an OCD component I truly had.

I spent months completing that list and exploring music libraries for anything related to what I had discovered. I moved to Santa Cruz, California, a couple of years later and eventually met Lou Harrison, one of America's foremost new music composers. He had been working on a similar idea for many years, and we spent an afternoon sharing thoughts on how the fundamental rhythm patterns could be explored.

Harrison encouraged me to take it as far as I could, which led to me moving to Washington D.C. in 1987 to use the Library of Congress to do further research. It took many years, but in 2012, I finally completed my comprehensive rhythm pattern theory resource, *The Elements of Rhythm, Vols. I & II*. It remains the toughest writing challenge I've ever faced, and it taught me that if you push hard and work smart enough, you really *can* do anything.

But honestly, I think the strangest turn in the road occurred while living in Washington. I landed a job working for a government contractor involved with Coast Guard aviation, where we developed their first electronic version of a helicopter flight manual (HH-65A, the model made popular in the 1980's TV series, *Baywatch*). I was inputting edits from the tech writers, and the more I looked at the manual, I became convinced that there was also a lot more going into maintaining the safety of aircraft than I had ever imagined.

When I learned that ALL aircraft were maintained using such detailed procedures, I decided to check out general aviation by taking a demo flight in a small, two-seater airplane, a Cessna 152. After the first ten seconds of lifting off out of Baltimore-Washington International airport, I was instantly hooked on small airplanes. I mean, *hooked!*

It took a year and half to convince the FAA that I was safe and did not require medication, but eventually, they issued me a special issuance FAA medical certificate. From there, I went on to earn my private, instrument, commercial, flight instructor, and instrument flight instructor ratings.

I've since flown over 8,000 hours, sending many people on to test for and earn their wings, with much of that time spent in the skies over Los Angeles. And believe me, on more than one occasion, having Tourette's was *exactly* what I needed to keep pace with so much happening so fast.

So, yes... it's been a pretty intense ride...

Epilogue

You recall that in the Introduction, I said I wanted to share how music has been of benefit in helping me cope with Tourette's. Coping is management of something, but the reality is this: we live with a neurological disability which as of this writing has no cure. It's not fair, and it changes everything.

So, we must change with it.

And we *can*.

Please remember this. We are not helpless victims. We are capable individuals with free will and powerful inner strength that can be tapped into for those times when the world dishes up more than we asked for. We do the best we can, and then, we rest and take on the next day. Living with Tourette's is very hard sometimes, and while music has helped me, it can only do so much... but because it *does* do so much, I really hope you will give it a try.

We need space now and then where we can go be whoever we are and whoever we need to be. We need freedom, the lack of walls, and time to ourselves to deal with this uninvited neurological visitor. As my friend, actress, and former TSA Youth Ambassador Hayley Gripp says, we can handle a lot and recharge our batteries if we can just get a break from things sometimes.

Everyone does this in their own way, and each of us needs to discover *what* that way is. For parents reading this book, I hope you will be able to create many opportunities for your children to freely explore music. A few lessons, an MP3 player, a smart pad or smart phone to get lost in, listening or dancing to live music... these are the pleasures and the escapes we crave.

For those of you with Tourette's, know this: ***you are not alone, and you do not have to be.*** Playing music with other people lets you become part of something fun, something where everyone is working together to make a beautiful sound. That effort can take you far away from the nervous movements and endless thoughts.

Want more proof? Ask jazz pianist Michael Wolff, composer Tobias Picker, classical pianist Nick van Bloss, guitarist Greg Kingston, singer/composer Nick Tatham, blues-rock guitarist Rick Fowler, singer/songwriter Magdalen Hsu-Li, guitarist Leonard W. Misner, songwriter Dave Brebner, poet/musician Vernon Frazer, classical music conductor Paige Vickery, music educator Michael Wickersham, composer/keyboardist Luke Parkin, British composer James McConnel, composer Jim Couchenour, keyboardist Bryan Randall Smith, drumming circle leader drummer Matt Giordano, singer James Durbin, singer/composer Jamie Grace, singer Rhianna Wicken...

And remember, regardless of which instrument(s) you choose to explore, or how young or old you are, go have fun! You don't have to be a pro, and don't worry about trying to sound perfect, because honestly, it doesn't matter.

All that *really* matters... is that you play.

Just play!

Tourette Syndrome and Music

photo by Lita D. Aldridge

photo by Julie Collier, Tourettes Action UK

About the Author

David R. Aldridge is a drummer, multi-instrumental musician, writer, publisher, educator/clinician, and airplane flight instructor, who has lived Tourette Syndrome for most of his life and has used music as therapy to deal with this disorder.

David has led drum set/drum circle demonstrations in the U.S. and the U.K., and his explorations of drumming as therapy have been documented in several publications, including the short story, "Rhythm Man," from **Don't Think About Monkeys** (Hope Press), *by Adam Ward Seligman and John S. Hilkevich*, and **Musicophilia: Tales of Music and the Brain** (Knopf Doubleday), by neurologist Oliver Sacks, M.D.

As a former freelance writer, David was a long-time contributor to *Drum!* magazine. He also wrote articles for *Modern Drummer, DownBeat, Jazziz,* and *Keyboard* magazines. Additionally, David is the author **The Elements of Rhythm, Vols. I & II** (Rollinson Publishing Co., 2012), a unique and comprehensive approach to rhythm pattern theory.

David also writes an on-going blog **(David Aldridge's Drumming Blog: Fuel for Rhythmic Thought)**, filled with notions on rhythm, Tourette's, drumming, and more.

Hope to see you there!

For current information about David's
live performances, drum set/drum circle demos,
and personal contact, please visit

www.davidaldridge.net

To follow David's drumming blog, please visit

davidaldridge.wordpress.com